Romance In The Old Folk's Home

Dr. Joanne Nelson King Brown

Copyright © 2011 by Dr. Joanne Nelson King Brown

Romance In The Old Folks Home
by Dr. Joanne Nelson King Brown

Printed in the United States of America

ISBN 9781613793145

All rights reserved solely by the author. The author guarantees all contents are original and do not infringe upon the legal rights of any other person or work. No part of this book may be reproduced in any form without the permission of the author. The views expressed in this book are not necessarily those of the publisher.

Unless otherwise indicated, Bible quotations are taken from The Living Bible. Copyright © 1971 by Tyndale Publishers, Inc. Used by permission.

www.xulonpress.com

5/28/11

Carol, God has put blessings all along your walk way here on earth. I pray you find each one, starting today. You were and are a blessing to me.

Joanne

Dedicated

To

    My

        Born

            Again

                Reiny

Preface

Thanks to all of you who prayed for me while I was writing this book. May it be a blessing to many.

Again I must thank my sons for all their help with this book. A computer dumb Mom has a hard time writing a book without a lot of help. Tim, thanks for bringing me down a new computer and printer. I can now sit in my recliner and write. Tom, thanks for answering my questions and helping me via the phone. Michael, thanks for your patience when I can't remember how to do something on the computer.

Thanks to Vicki for helping me remember who did what, when.

Thanks to Virginia for sharing her editing skills with me, while still allowing me to be me.

Thanks to God for allowing me to share Reiny with everyone else. As you will read, he was something else.

The Move

It was definitely not the wind rattling the front door. Someone obviously was trying to break in, but who would want to do that? For some strange reason I didn't feel afraid, but maybe I should have. As I pulled myself out of the big overstuffed chair to go see who it was, the phone rang.

"Hi, son! Yes, I was just resting from all that unpacking but my front door is rattling, and I don't think it is just the wind. It is kind of late for anyone to come calling, and I don't know anyone here yet anyway. Hang on; I'm going to open the door. Oh, it will be O K. If it's a bad guy, and he gets me, you can call the police. Don't hang up now." The fact that he was in Portland and I was 100 miles away meant nothing, right?

The cold night air swished past me into my cozy warm living room as I timidly opened the door and peeked out. There stood a well-dressed, good looking old man. A startled look crossed the old man's face and he began to back off the porch.

"Yes, how may I help you?" I yelled at the old man. Still not a word from him.

"Are you still there, son? That didn't take long. It was a man all right but he didn't say anything, not a word, just backed off the porch and started walking. He didn't seem to know where he was going so I just shut and locked the door. He was pretty good-looking too. I'll tell you more tomorrow, and yes, I will report it to the manager. Love you too. Bye, son."

I slumped down in my big overstuffed chair and wondered, *what was that all about?* I was exhausted and knew I should get myself to bed. There were still boxes to be unpacked from my move a few days ago, but they could wait until tomorrow. This moving business was getting harder and harder, and

I wasn't getting any younger. I hope this will be my last move. This active, independent, gracious living, retirement home that I had just moved into, seemed nice enough, and I liked the people I'd met so far.

I knew my grandkids would be coming any day now. They would help me with the unpacking. So I pulled myself out of the chair and headed for my bed.

When I awoke the next morning, every bone in my body ached. I really wanted to just sleep in, but breakfast was served at 8 o'clock. I had no groceries in the cottage I had rented. Therefore, I had better get myself showered and dressed and trot across the parking lot to the main building where the meals were being served. (I'm using the term "trot" loosely, you understand!) I am an old lady, but not as old as some here. To live to be 100 seems very attainable here.

It was a little intimidating to think about making new friends at my age, but I really had no choice.

Bravely I opened my front door at 7:50 a.m. and stepped out. I was so glad it was not raining. As I was living in Salem, Oregon, I should expect lots of rain. It just comes with the territory. I had just walked down my little sidewalk and reached the parking lot when a strong male voice yelled.

"Hey, wait up!"

The voice was coming from the porch just 2 doors down from me. *I think that is the man that was at my door last night.* I did wait for him.

"Did you get the wrong house last night?"

I smiled at him but really, I didn't bat my eyelashes, (too much.)

"Yes,"

He smiled back and put his arm on my shoulder, then continued,

"but there isn't a court in the land that would convict me for trying to break into such a beautiful ladies' house."

Oh my, this man has a silver tongue. I better watch out for him. His arm across my shoulder was feeling very good. It had been a few years since I had had the warmth of an arm on my shoulder. I hated for us to reach the main building but it really wasn't very far across the parking lot.

I thought, *good, I'll have someone to sit with.* But as we entered the dining room he headed for a table that only had one seat left. His daughters had picked out that table for him when they had eaten there the day before. He sat down and apparently I was forgotten (or ignored). He had a lady former senator sitting with him. She seemed very nice. Also there was another lady and another man. The tables would only seat four. We weren't assigned seats to eat but most of the residents sat at the same table every meal. They didn't like you to sit in 'their' chair. Not too far away there was another table with an empty chair and I plopped down. It turned out to be the table where another neighbor, Eleanor, usually sat. She lived on the opposite end from where my new male neighbor lived. We were soon chatting and laughing like old friends. Eleanor was a jewel and I grew to love her dearly. I could feel eyes on me, so turned around. My silver tongued neighbor was looking at me, but looked away quickly when I turned around. The next time he looked at me, I winked, and then I didn't turn around again. Now you may think that I am a flirt.

You're probably right. Old age does come with some privileges.

I was just getting up to go back to my cottage when over *'he'* came. He introduced himself to Eleanor and me and we told him our names. He had put his arm on my shoulder but had not introduced himself yet. His name was Reiny. Apparently he was going to walk me home as he stayed right by my shoulder. I figured he probably knew his way home by now, but, just in case, I'd let him walk me home, and he did.

That noon at lunch (or dinner as they call it) we had a lady walking around the tables playing her accordion. She was playing a Polka just as Reiny, my new neighbor, came into the dining area. He used his walking stick for balance and began to Polka down the center aisle, between the tables. He was good. I had no idea how to Polka, so felt my chances with him were nil.

First Date Or No Date?

That night I watched him drive out of the parking lot. I wondered where he went. At 10:15 he pulled in again and I peeked out the curtain and watched him. He looked over at my door, but then went on into his own cottage.

The next morning he came to walk me to breakfast again and I found out he went dancing at the Senior Center the night before. That sounded like lots of fun but wondered how he could dance as he used a stick cane to walk steadily. He invited me to go dancing with him the next time, but I declined.

When I told my kids and grandkids I had been invited to go dancing they all agreed that I should accept the invitation and go. After several more invitations, I surprised us both, and accepted. I was excited as I loved to dance.

When the night came, one of my table mates, Ginny, advised me to be sure and take money along as I might need to call a taxi to come home, in case he was an axe murderer or something. I did take her advice.

I was so excited! That evening, after dinner, I got ready and hurried over to his cottage. I timidly knocked on his door. When he answered he looked surprised. I was puzzled and said shyly,

"I'm here to go dancing with you."

"But we don't leave for an hour yet."

He informed me. He did not invite me in. How embarrassing! Now he would think I was sure anxious to go with him. This time it was me who backed off the porch and headed to my cottage. Was my face red!

Well, I'll just stay home tonight and watch T V and forget this dancing stuff with a total stranger. But at the proper time I had a knock on my door and there he stood.

"I know you're ready so let's go."

Now if that isn't romantic, I don't know what is.

His smile was just too inviting so I weakened and went with him. He opened the car door as a nice gentleman and again smiled so nicely at me. I began to feel comfortable again. It didn't take us long to get there and soon he was opening my door to walk to the building. It was such a lovely night, the walk to the center from the parking lot was oh, so pleasant, and he again put his arm around my shoulder. He hadn't even held my hand yet but had put his arm around my shoulder twice. Hummmmmm!

As he opened the senior center door he whispered in my ear and said,

"Did you bring any money?"

I looked up at him startled and wondered if this was not a date but he had just offered to drive me to the senior center dance?

"Yes!" I replied rather crisply.

"Good, as it costs $3.00 to get in."

I couldn't believe my ears. I marched down the hall and into the open door to the dance hall, walked in, and put down a $10.00 bill.

"Do you want to pay for his ticket too?" she insistently asks?

"No!"

I took my change and found a seat. He was on his own and I would be too. He came over and sat with me. I just ignored him and started talking and making friends with the couple on the other side of our table. Before I could blink my eye he had a lady walking over to him and held out her hand to him to dance with her. He turned to me and asks,

"Do you mind?"

"Of course not, go right ahead."

I felt that I certainly had no claim on him. He was just my chauffeur. I figured the ladies were all probably mad at me for showing up with their favorite dance partner anyway.

I visited with the nice couple across the table. They were getting married in a few months and were so happy. They had met at the center a few months ago.

Reiny came back, but as soon as the next piece started another woman came rushing over to him. This was a polka and I knew he loved to dance the polka and I didn't know how.

"Yes, of course, have fun!"

It was fun watching him dance and he did really well without his walking stick. He told me the first time he came dancing here he fell down as he tried to dance without the aid of his stick, but got up and practiced and now felt pretty secure.

"Here comes another lady but please say 'No' this time. I'd like to ask you to dance with me." Reiny pleaded.

He grabbed for my hand to lift me off the chair and I gladly went with him. I hung on pretty tight at first to keep my balance, but eventually was swaying nicely to the music and smiling up at him. This was really kind of fun. I liked it.

We both got winded but stayed out on the floor for the next song, thus avoiding woman coming over to get him. He was a good looking man, and by far the best looking man in the whole place. He was a sharp dresser and never looked sloppy. He wore tight fitting western pants, as oppose to slacks. He wore a vest most of the time, which looked really good as he was slim and well built.

Reiny had an air about him like he knew what he wanted, and would get it. Yet you didn't feel he was stuck up.

About 9:00 woman starting putting food out on the tables, and the dancers all lined up to eat.

"Do you want anything?" Reiny asks.

"Yes, I'd like a drink of ice tea, please"

"O. K. let's get up and get in line."

With my arthritic knees, standing in line is not easy, but I was determined to do it, and I did. This was strike two for him as he should have gotten my drink for me. One more strike and Reiny would be out.

He filled a plate with the food that was spread out, but I wasn't hungry.

After he ate we decided to go home as it was almost 10:00.

He brought my coat out of the coat closet and helped me put it on. That was a plus point for him. As we walked out to the car the moon was out so pretty and it was a lovely night. The ride home was quiet as we were both tired. When he pulled in front of his cottage, I patted his arm, thanked him, then jumped out and walked the 2 doors down to my place. I unlocked my door and never looked back his way.

As I wrote in my journal that night, I decided that was the strangest date that I had ever been on before. I did like him. He was from North Dakota and maybe that explained why he was different than what I was used to. *I will just have to see what happens next*, I wrote.

I Think He Likes Me

The next morning when I stepped out to go to breakfast I almost knocked him down as he was standing on my porch, ready to escort me to the dining room. He had such a big smile on his face.

"I apologize for letting you pay last night. Please don't tell anyone."

"Oh, no! That's the first thing I'm going to do. Ginny told me to take money and I'm going to tell her it's a good thing I did."

"Would you go with me again and this time I'll pay and we can go out to dinner or at least get something to eat afterwards?"

"Let me think about it. You are a good dancer, and I really do enjoy your company."

The ladies at the table wanted to know all about my evening out. I had fun telling them. I spoke softly so as not to embarrass Reiny too much.

He walked me over to breakfast each morning until one day when it was pouring rain and I waited and waited but no Reiny. I decided to give him a call and see if he was ill.

"Oh, hi! No, I went the side door today as it is closer for me. I'll come get you though. Wait for me."

Before I could put the phone in my pocket he was on my front step with his hand out to help me off the porch. He grabbed my umbrella and held it over us as we scooted across the parking lot. The rain dripped down my collar as he was taller than I and held the umbrella over his head. After that he never ever missed taking me to breakfast again, rain, shine, sleet, snow or ice. When it became real icy he used his walker and had me hold on to him. As my arthritis got worse he would say,

"Just hop on my back and I'll carry you across."

This made me laugh as I was no tiny thing. I later found out he probably could have done it as he was used to carrying big rolls of roofing up ladders.

Reiny made life such fun. One morning someone had put a huge bouquet of real flowers by the fireplace where we ate. They were probably left over from a funeral. I hung up my coat and headed into the dining area when I heard this lovely voice singing………..

"Here she comes. Miss America"

Reiny came singing toward me thru the tables with a beautiful rose from the bouquet and presented it to me with a big bow and smile. I felt so special. What a neat way to start the day. He walked me home and we stood and laughed and talked outside my door, even though it was only 19 degrees out there.

I awoke to lots of snow on a day that I had to get my mother from her nursing home in Turner,(the next town southeast of where I lived,) and take her to the doctor two towns over. Not a fun trip. That Doctor sent us to Portland, almost 100 miles away. Again it was not a fun trip. Spent all day and wearily headed home at nightfall. Snow was just beginning to float down. The doctors at O H S U decided mother did not have an emergency.

My cell phone had 3 messages on it from Reiny. He was worried about me. How sweet. It seemed awfully nice to have someone care about you. I decided to talk to Tim's wife, Tami, about "age differences," I knew she was quite a bit younger than my son and was eager to get her opinion. I knew I was a lot younger than Reiny but so far it didn't seem to matter one little bit.

"Maybe Reiny is God's gift to you, Mom. We really like him."

That would mean, of course, that I was God's gift to Reiny too. It gave me something to think about.

That night my lady friends were not at supper and Reiny ask me to sit with him. We had a laughing good time. He told me about himself. Said he had had 3 wives. He had two daughters living in the area and 2 sons in Washington State. He was very proud of them all. He was very proud of all of his grandkids and great grandkids too. He would love to show me pictures of them sometime, he said.

He had an identical twin who had died a short time ago. His twin had been ill at the V A hospital, when he died. Soon after his twin died Reiny went to sign up at the same V A hospital. Everyone there seemed so shocked when they saw Reiny. They mistook him for his twin brother.

"We thought you had died!"

"I decided to come back" he told them.

They thought they were seeing a ghost. He had a funny sense of humor.

His parents were Germans who lived in Russia and fled to the United States thru Ellis Island to escape religious persecution. They migrated out to the Dakotas with lots of other German friends. As they spoke only German in his home and his mother could not speak English at all, Reiny was really at a disadvantage when he started the 1ˢᵗ grade. He said the teacher hit him a lot because he didn't do what she said, but he had no idea what she was asking of him.

He told me he loved to dance the Polka, play Poker, gamble and drink. Oh my,my! What was the Lord giving me?

I decided to give him my first book I had written about when I was a missionary in the jungles of South America, and see what he thought.

The next day Reiny sat with Ginny at breakfast and did not eat with me or walk with me. I guessed that my book scared him off.

The next day snow and ice covered the parking lot that we had to cross to get to the main building. I sadly and cautiously started alone across the slippery parking lot. Then I heard a male voice behind me yelling,

"I'll help you across the slippery ice."

"You want to slip with me?" I replied.

Then I realized if you were hard of hearing that might sound like something else. He did wear hearing aids.

Reiny was coming toward me across the ice, using his walker. I hung onto him, and he hung onto his walker. We made it just fine.

I Think I Like Him

I was settling into my big chair after supper that same night when there was a knock on my door. I had just noticed that Reiny had driven in. Sure enough it was him.

"May I come in and talk?"

"Sure," I said, and stepped aside to allow him to pass.

There was only one place two people could sit in my little living room, and that was the davenport. I didn't know if I wanted to get that friendly but I did sit down very prim and proper like. I even had the folded hands on my lap.

He sat down next to me prim and proper like too. He wanted my second book to read as well. He had passed on my first book to his daughter to read. Of course, I gave him a copy.

We seemed to have no trouble visiting nor did we run out of anything to say. When my mother called at 9:00, as she usually did, and found out I had a visitor, she said,

"You better send him home now."

I really laughed as not many women my age have a mother telling them to send a man home.

My mother had passed the 100 mark and was very proud of it. In the days to come when the phone rang around 9:00 Reiny would laugh and say,

"Tell your mother I'm going out the door now."

The next day Reiny seemed very distant. He was reading my second book so I felt he wasn't really interested in a woman like me. It made me sad as every day I liked him more and more. We seemed to have so much fun together. Well, I knew whatever the Lord had planned was O K with me.

Valentine's Day was coming up and I found a cute "neighbor" card. I thought I could give it to him. Meanwhile Ginny and I traveled on the retirement home's bus up to I Max for the day. We got home after supper. As soon as I entered my cottage the phone rang.

"I missed you at supper."

He did care!

"I will be gone to my grandkids for a while." He informed me, "but I'll call you!"

How nice of him to let me know. I went to bed with a smile on my face. He was such a nice man. I wondered where all this would lead?

A Real Date and A Real Hug

"I would like you to go with me to a concert where my son in law is singing tonight. Would you go? My daughter is bringing me tickets at noon today."

Well, it's not exactly the way I would have asked someone but I was beginning to feel more comfortable with his way of saying things. He didn't leave anything to guess work and that was nice. I knew his heart was in the right place.

"Yes, I would like that. Thank you! When should I be ready?"

"We'll leave at 7:00."

His daughter's car was parked in front of his cottage so he hurried off. As she was leaving she veered over to me and opened her window, introduced herself and then asks,

"Why do you like my Dad?"

Wow! That took me a bit by surprise. I had not really stopped to think about it. Why did I like Reiny?

"Your Daddy is a real charmer!" I left it at that.

That night, at seven sharp, Reiny was at my door and he escorted me to his car. The program was very enjoyable. At intermission his son in law came and introduced himself to me. He certainly seemed nice. After the program Reiny ask if I wanted anything to eat.

"How much money do you have?" I teased him.

"No, not really," I answered him seriously, "but thanks, probably another time."

This time when we got home he grabbed my hands and brought them up to his lips and kissed them, before I scooted out my side of the car and on to my cottage. I did thank him as I slid out the SUV door.

Valentine's Day was here and Reiny and I sat together and laughed and had a good time. He invited me to his house after supper so I gave him the "neighbor" Valentine card and some mints I had for him. We watched T V, visited, laughed, and petted (the dog that is). His dog, "Buddy," was very jealous of me, as he was used to having Reiny all to himself. I gave Buddy his treat and he felt better about me. As I am very allergic to cats and dogs I began to stuff up after a short while and knew it was time to leave. When I got up to leave Reiny put his arms around me and gave me a very strong loving hug. Oh, he was a good hugger. That was certainly a plus, as I loved hugs.

The next day Reiny gave me the keys to his place as he was going on the retirement home's bus to the casino for the day and I would let Buddy out and give him a treat and visit with him. I did just that.

Reiny called me several times during the day and we laughed and had such fun conversations. I wondered if I might be depending on him too much for my "feel goodness?" I wondered what he thought about our relationship.

Reiny liked to get his hair cut from Carol, a beautician where we lived. I could see why. She was breath taking pretty, with long beautiful hair. I had heard that when he got his hair cut he had told Carol that he was falling in love.

"Who with?" she asked, surprised. She had no idea.

"Joanne, my neighbor." He grinned.

Reiny went to his daughter's that night and I did miss him. I wondered what he would tell them about us. He had just kissed my hand and given me a couple of hugs, so far. His daughter told me later that he told his kids, when he first moved in,

"I don't like it here. Look around. There's just a bunch of old people."

"But Dad, you're old too." They reminded him. (He was just pushing 90)

The next day he walked me to breakfast and afterward stopped by and talked, and talked. That night he brought his daughter over to visit, and I went back over to his place for left over restaurant food, heated in the micro.

"Would you like to see my family?"

"Yes, I would"

So I settled down on his davenport with my legs curled up beside me. Not prim and proper at all. He hauled out albums and boxes of pictures. My, his twin did look like him. He had pictures of his first wife and third wife but none of the second one. I ask why and he replied,

"I never should have married her. My friends just kept pushing me until I did. It was never a happy time."

I took that to mean the case was closed. I was not to ask any more about that, so I didn't. He seemed to have a lot in his past that he didn't want to talk about and that he wished he didn't have. I wondered how or if I would fit into his future?

What will Blue Ice Lead to?

What is that thing on my porch leaning against the post? I squinted to see as I parked my car. I began to laugh as I approached the porch and saw a cute 1 foot chocolate rabbit waiting for me. It was only Feb.22nd so I would have plenty of time to eat it before the Easter season was over. I might even share it with the giver.

That giver also wanted to give me some "Blue Ice" gel for my arthritic knees. He brought some over and wanted me to put it on RIGHT NOW. So I went into the bathroom and rubbed some on. It did feel good but didn't last too long.

"You probably didn't put it on right. Let me rub it on you." Now that was very sweet of him but what he didn't realize is that my pant legs were too skinny to be able to pull them up above my knees in order to rub the gel on. I was not about to drop my slacks, expose my under panties, just so he could rub my knee.

"Joanne wouldn't let me rub her knee!" he later complained to his daughter.

She probably thought her Dad had really gotten himself mixed up with a prude. Later when she told me what Reiny had said, I laughed and explained to her what happened.

It was very thoughtful of him to give me the jar of gel. Sure made the wearer stink. My new perfume, I guessed.

After supper Reiny came over and hiked up his trousers and showed me how he felt I ought to put the gel onto my knees. I wanted to laugh so badly but kept myself in check and just thanked him so much. If he could stand the smell of me I guess it was O K but I didn't feel I wanted to wear that perfume to church or ladies' meetings.

Reiny did not walk me to breakfast because it was raining very hard. Then he apologized all day long. He called twice in the evening as he went dancing alone. I know the ladies at the senior center were happy I was not there. My arthritis was so bad, I was glad I was not there, too.

The next day Reiny called and invited me to go dancing with him and have dinner afterwards. I probably should have gone but I really feel he likes his independence and likes dancing with all the ladies. I feel I cramp his style with the ladies. So I just stayed home and watched T V. I did notice when he came pulling in his parking place and it wasn't even 10 yet. I peeked out my window. He looked at my door for quite some time but then walked on in his house. I could hear Buddy barking so he no doubt felt he better go in and tend to him.

I turned off my lights and ran to the back bedroom so if he took the dog out, he wouldn't stop at my door. The next morning when he came to walk me to breakfast he said,

"I saw your light on when I pulled up and was tempted to come over when I took the dog out, even if you had turned off your lights."

He grabbed my hand and held it tightly all the way across the parking lot. *What a man,* I thought

"Now, Joanne, the next time you have to take your mother somewhere let me come with you and help you deal with her wheel chair. That's too heavy for you to lift into the trunk of your car."

What a thoughtful man. I think I am kind of falling for this guy. After supper he walked me home then later called me and said

"I haven't talked to you in 20 minutes. I miss you"

He makes me smile and laugh a lot.

The next evening Reiny and I ate alone. I discovered he was a good conversationalist. He told me about the visit to Austria he took with his eldest daughter, Vicki. He had had a very good time. He helped me on with my coat and we trudged home thru the rain.

Later on that evening, after I had changed to my night clothes, and put on my housecoat, there was a knock on my door.

"Do you think my key would work in your door?" He yelled from my porch.

"No, you've already tried that the first night you were here." I reminded him. I did open the door and he came in and headed for the davenport.

He told me he didn't want to leave me this summer but was planning to go back to North Dakota to a family reunion. He also told me,

"My daughter is going to redesign my place and I told her I could just stay with my neighbor." (He meant me) I just laughed and said,

"I don't think so!"

He got up to go home and I got off the davenport to see him out. He grabbed me and gave me a big hug. Oh, I liked that. I really like hugs. It had been five months and he had not kissed me yet but I had had two big hugs. He was a head taller than I and was very strong. I liked that too. I wondered if this relationship was going anywhere or if we would just be good friends for life? I'm sure that's what his kids would like, but I wasn't sure that's what he wanted. Later on my mother would say,

"Why do you have to marry him? Why not just be friends?" Obviously she had forgotten how wonderful it was to fall asleep in someone's arms, or wake up to a smiling face looking at you. Or hear

"I love you" as the first words of the day.

"The Kiss"

After an exhausting day of taking mother to Eugene (some 60 miles away) to a luncheon at the college to honor those who gave scholarships, I finally pulled into my parking place at my cottage. Home never looked so good.

I barely made it in the door when Reiny came over carrying beautiful Easter lilies. I was so happy! I wanted some Easter lilies, and nearly did buy some, when I was at the store with mother. I was so glad I hadn't. Flowers always made me smile.

My son, Mike, called and said Reiny had to fill out a 100 questionnaire before he could bring me anymore flowers. My boys were beginning to notice that ' Mom had a man in her life.'

I tumbled into bed and was just drifting off to sleep, when the phone rang.

"Your mother has a high fever and needs to go to the hospital," the nurse at Turner, informed me.

I dragged myself out of bed, dressed and headed over to the next town. I couldn't see on Turner road as it was black and rainy. Kind of spooky, so I just started to sing praises to my God , and made it fine.

By 2:30 a.m. I could hardly stay awake in the E R room.

"Lord, I need some help here!" I pleaded.

Just then the curtain was pulled back and someone came in and handed me a container of orange juice, and a package of crackers. I thanked them and smiled. *I believe I just saw an angel,* I said to myself. Finally at 3:30 a. m. I was headed with mother back to Turner.

Before I jumped into bed I put a note on my door letting Reiny know that I hoped I was sleeping when he usually came knocking. He did not wake me.

That afternoon my friend Vesta picked me up and took me to her women's Christian group from church. It was nice. When I got home Reiny was right over there to walk me to supper and ask me out to a movie afterwards.

Even though I was tired; I did want to go with him so we left right away and saw "The Bucket List". I noticed, to my delight, that in an exceptionally emotional part, Reiny had tears in his eyes. I'm glad he is a feeling man even though he likes to appear rough and tough. He held my hand all the way through the movie.

He has such a big hand, it completely covers mine. Hmmmmm nice!

Outside the movie house we saw a former manager that we both knew and liked. She was shocked Reiny and I were together. We visited for a while then headed home.

When we got home he walked me into my cottage but I didn't ask him to stay. He gently removed my coat and laid it on the big chair then put his arms around me. He put one of his big hands behind my head and neck and bent over until our lips met. I could not pull away if I had wanted to, which I did not want to do. I did not realize how many good feeling nerve endings God had put in the lips. Reiny was hitting them all. I could feel his kiss clear to my toes.

Finally he released my head and brought his lips to my ear via my neck and said,

"I've wanted to do that for a long time! Now I don't want to go home. I love you, sweetheart."

We were both startled out of our romantic mood by my phone ringing. We looked at my phone in the chair and there was Mom's name in the display window. I thought he was going to grab it and through it in the middle of the street, so I reached down and threw it over onto the davenport, then as sweetly and gently as possible pushed him out the door.

As soon as the door was shut I let out a big "Whoopee!" I walked over to where I kept my 1st and 2nd husband's pictures setting, and removed them from their places and took them back to my bedroom. Reiny's and my relationship had moved to another level.

The next evening when Reiny came over to watch T V he immediately noticed that John's and Dale's pictures were gone. Also, I had moved my wedding ring to my right hand.

As we sat watching T V his hands began to wander where they didn't yet belong, so I gently put his arm up around my shoulder, smiled my sweetest and said

"You need a piece of paper to go there, sweetheart."

He behaved himself until the next commercial then he sat bolt upright and started looking all around, like he lost something.

"What are you looking for?"

"A piece of paper" he grinned.

Rings

"Would you go to the Mall with me today, honey," Reiny ask as he put some coffee down for me at 7:00 a.m. That was the start of his coffee run that lasted every day until I moved. As we lived across the parking lot from the big house we were always being watched.

"I hope they see me coming over at night and then see me leave after coffee in the morning," he said hopefully. He wanted to appear as a bad boy.

Most of the residents knew I would not allow that, but I didn't spoil his hopes.

We walked into the mall holding hands and he headed straight for a jewelry shop. He asks to see wedding rings. Oh, they showed us beautiful ones. We both spied the same one at the same time that seemed just perfect for me. The engagement ring fit into the wedding ring and made a beautiful pair. He found one he liked for himself and started to pay for them all.

"No, I'm supposed to buy yours!"

"You don't have to, I'm so happy to be engaged to you I'd buy my own ring."

I did buy his ring, even though I had not yet been asked to marry him. He waited until they were sized and then when we picked them up he came over to the house, knelt on one knee, told me he loved me and asked if I would show him the paper, and we could both sign it. He was so cute. I had to laugh.

"I've never had a proposal like that before!"

I accepted his proposal and he got off his knee (with help) and then helped me up and I got my second wonderful kiss. It was better than the first one but I sure didn't know how that could be. Did I mention he was a good kisser?

Running Away From Home!

It was not yet light as I crept quietly as possible out my door and silently to my neighbor's. I slipped an envelope in his screen door and hoped the dog didn't hear me. Then I jumped in my car and drove off.

I had not slept all night thinking about what I had done. I loved this nice neighbor man but he was 15 years older than I and so very different than any man I had ever known. We could probably have

10 years of marriage at the most. Could I stand the pain of losing him? Could I make him happy? I knew I needed to write him a note:

"Dearest Reiny,

You are an honest man; therefore, I must be honest too. I fear there is just too big a gap in our ages. You are a different generation than I. I feel our marriage would be too difficult in the long run.

I thought that when I fell head over heels in love with you that it was surely God's making.

Thank you for all your kind words to me. Kindness is so sexy to a woman. You are a wonderful man but not the one for me.

I will take the rings back and I have enclosed a check for the amount. I am leaving town for a while to think. Sorry, I am too embarrassed to tell you this in person.

>Your former love and now X fiancée"

I could not remember writing another "dear John" letter. I put a check for my ring in the envelope. It was Easter morning and I knew he would be embarrassed as he was supposed to take me to a family Easter dinner and introduce me to all his family.

Later his kids told me he just said, when they ask where I was, that he and I had 'hit a bump in the road'. What a nice way to put it.

I headed south not really knowing where I was going but I knew I had to be alone with God and do some soul searching. I was feeling so confused as I pulled into Safeway for gas.

"What are you doing up so early on Easter morning?" the attendant questioned me.

"I'm running away from home. I have some thinking to do."

"Don't go too far so you can't come back!"

That sounded like good advice to me. I thought about that as I headed out south on I-5. I stopped and got my mocha and toast at a favorite restaurant at the Corvallis turn off.

Why not go to my old church with my very dear friend and get lots of hugs today, I thought. My car knew the way by heart and my fate for the day was sealed. First I went to a sister retirement home to see if they had a guest room available for the night. They did and a lovely one at that. My friend, Pat, and I could eat Easter dinner here too.

Pat, was helping at the LaSalle center, on the O S U campus, where the service was being held. I went in and saved her a place and meanwhile collected hugs from all my old Corvallis friends. I got hugs from some that weren't old too. This was indeed a good idea.

I took time out to call my friend, Ginny, back in Salem, and tell her,

"I've run away from home but will be back tomorrow"

I didn't want her to worry.

It was a lovely Easter service and we sang the familiar Easter songs. I was enjoying it and losing myself completely. Afterwards Pat & I had a great time laughing and talking over the excellent meal at the retirement home where I was staying.

Then it was time for me to be alone. I could see on my phone where Reiny had called three times already. I knew I was not going to call him until I got back to Salem the next day.

I dug out some paper and drew a line down the middle. One side was marked *pro* and the other *con*. Then I ask the Lord to direct my thinking as I filled in the two columns of the paper. After about an hour I got up and walked around. I found the exercise equipment the facility had and got on a machine and worked out for a half hour. After supper I brought out the paper again and began to look it over.

It seemed the Pro side was very long and the Con side only had one thing on it. Reiny's age! His mind was sharp; his health was good as could be expected for his age. How important was age? I loved the guy. Soooooooooooooooooo, it was decided! I would go back and if he still wanted me (after me running away and embarrassing him,) he would be stuck with me for life. Having decided my future I fell into bed and slept like a baby until the sun came up.

I pulled back onto I-5 and headed north. I was scared. Reiny was a perfectionist and wondered if he could handle the fact that I was far from one. My first husband was also a perfectionist and soon was buying two tubes of tooth paste, one for each of us to squeeze. I always squeezed the tube just anywhere, middle, top or bottom. He put up with my sloppiness in the kitchen and offered to clean up after me. My second husband was also a perfectionist and bought two tubes of tooth paste. He too said," You make the mess in the kitchen and I will clean it up. Now, how would this Reiny re-act to my non perfect ways?

I pulled into Shari's restaurant and found a seat by the front window, pulled out my phone and dialed him. He picked the phone up on the first ring and said,

"Hello, Sweetheart!"

I was a goner! I told him where I was and almost before I hung up the phone; his car was swinging into the parking lot. He literally ran into the restaurant. Now this was some feat, as he usually always used his walking stick. I had never seen him actually run, before. I had gotten out of the booth by this time and he grabbed me, swung me around, put me down and gave me a big bear hug and kiss.

"Honey, I think we are the entertainment for the breakfast crew. We better sit down." I slid into the booth.

He sat next to me, not across from me, as if he wanted to make sure I didn't disappear again.

"Don't ever leave me again. I love you and missed you and worried about you."

I apologized and asked his forgiveness, and told him he was stuck with me from then on. He got out my check for the ring and tore it up, then handed me the pieces.

The next order of business would be to plan a wedding and buy two tubes of tooth paste.

Getting To Know Each Other Better

It was only 6:00 a.m. and I heard my front door rattling. I quickly threw on my old bathrobe and half asleep, staggered out to the living room and opened the door.

Reiny came in and set the coffee down, looked me over, and said," Is that what you look like first thing in the morning?"

"Exactly" I sleepily said.

He put his hands on his hips,

"Well, I think I can live with that," he grinned. Then as he went back out the door he turned and said,

"You better hurry; you only have two hours 'til you have to go over to breakfast."

I think he was implying that I might need more time than that to get myself presentable to be seen in public.

I grabbed a cup of his coffee, added my chocolate, and headed for the bedroom. As I passed a mirror on the way, I peeked at myself, and began to laugh. While I slept, my hair had squished itself all up on top of my head, like a kewpie doll.

I fluffed up my pillows, jumped back into bed to enjoy my mocha, and have my devotions. I laughed and thought, *if he can't handle what I looked like………..too bad! It serves him right for coming over so early.*

The next day he was back on his 7:00 a m coffee run. I think we both liked that better.

That night he came over to watch T V and we got all hot and bothered on the davenport. He told me how much he loved me. Now I knew, due to a botched cancer prostate operation, he no longer could hold intercourse, but his head did not seem to get the message. The results of his operation did not bother me, as I loved hugs and kisses. He was very good at both.

Preparing for the Future Together

On St Patrick's Day, we went to a concert and heard Irish songs. It was very good. Reiny told me several times that he loved me. I told him once. He told me he would be true to me "till death."

I think we could have a fun life together. Reiny wants to go "Motor Home" shopping. He has a motor home to trade in. It is stored at his grandson's place in Washington. He wants to take me up to see it soon. That would be a good idea.

The next day, Reiny picked me up before breakfast. We ate out; then went Motor Home shopping. We found a perfect one, not too short and not too long with several slide outs. It looked plenty big enough for the two of us to live in. It was only 28 feet long, but at our age, that was just right. It was a year old and used but still smelled and looked brand new. The couple had traded it in on a bigger one. I knew how that went. Everyone gets 2 foot itis. Every year you want one two feet longer than you have. They were only asking $75,000.

It only took me 30 minutes to get him down to $50,000, and he would allow $ 25,000 sight unseen (except for our picture of it) for Reiny's R V. I would pay the $25,000 difference. Reiny and he wanted us to sign, but I said,

"No, I need to pray about this first, if it's sold when we come back I'll know it was not for us."

That night when I prayed about the R V, I felt I was getting a

"No"

Well, I knew the Lord knew what the future held and I didn't, so I trusted Him.

We didn't get the R V. That was a good thing as the future unfolded as it did.

Reiny came over early to take me to lunch and wanted to stay and talk.

"Of course, come on in."

He said, "I just told my two daughters that I was getting married. They couldn't believe me!"

They probably wondered why?

I e mailed my three boys and told them. All they wanted to know was," Are you in love, mom?"

I told them,

"Yes, I was in love and falling more and more in love each day. Actually we feel like teenagers in love,"

"Friendship (love) doubles your joy and divides your grief." We both felt this Swedish proverb was true in our case.

Starting Wedding Plans

On the first day of spring, Reiny went with his grandkids to the casino. He didn't win anything but called me twice. Said he missed me so much he wasn't enjoying himself. When he got home he brought them over and introduced them to me. They seemed very nice. He seemed eager to tell them good- by so he could come over and spend the rest of the evening with me.

"Let's talk about the wedding." He said as he put his arm around me. "My son in law could marry us in my daughter's back yard. We could do it this week. We can get our license tomorrow. I don't want a big crowd because I might embarrass myself, because of my hearing problem."

"I love your enthusiasm but let me check out the church where I go. It has a chapel."

The next day we headed toward the city of Eugene to look at some more Motor Homes; but stopped for breakfast on the way and decided to turn back and not go there at all. We went to visit my mother instead.

While in Turner at Mother's we found a duplex for rent at just the price we wanted to pay. It was the very same one I had rented about a year ago. It had two bedrooms, a big living room, big kitchen, and a two door bathroom, plus a garage. It had plenty of storage space. My freezer was still in the garage and my washer dryer were in the bathroom. We put some money down on the duplex.

"We can put our furniture in this house, and us too, when we aren't traveling." Reiny was enthused!

The next day I drove to my church and learned they were charging even the members for the use of the chapel for weddings. I didn't like that, and dropped the idea.

While at Turner I was talking with the associate director of the home and she asked if Reiny and I would like to be the first couple to get married in the new Gazebo by the little river. It was just dedicated and was beautiful. I knew it could be decorated with flowers and be very pretty. Mother's room overlooked the area and that would be convenient for dressing and waiting. We would have to rent some chairs and as it was very hot in July. We would probably need a tent also for shade.

There would be no charge for us to use the Gazebo. We wanted to do something for them as a thank you, so as they didn't have a sound system, we decided to buy one for them. We would be the first ones to use it at our wedding.

We wanted to have my middle son, Tom, and Reiny's son- in- law, Maur, to share together in performing the marriage. He would pick his grandson, Andy, for his best man, and I would pick my eldest son, Tim, to give me away. My youngest son, Michael would sing. Reiny thought Mike had such a beautiful voice. Reiny ask another of his grandsons, Josh, to take the pictures. Which he did, and they turned out so good. We were very happy.

A dear friend from church, Allison, was willing to play the piano. I laughed when she threatened to play the "stripper" music as I came down the aisle.

As my sister was pregnant at my first wedding she couldn't be my maid of honor, and she was not in the area for the second one. I was happy now she could finally be my maid of honor. The wedding plans seemed to all be coming together nicely, then something happened that threatened to spoil it all.

Pain

My back pain became worse each day. The pain seemed to go down my leg. I had a yearly physical coming up, so I figured I'd mention my upcoming marriage and my crippling back ache. The two just didn't seem to go together.

After taking the M R I test to determine what was going on in my back, the doctor referred me to a specialist.

I sat in the specialist's office and thought, *if I am going to be like this the rest of my days; I better not get married and saddle* someone *with such a burden as I would be.*

The specialist informed me my spine was indeed full of arthritis. I would need several rods put into my back. The recovery period would take 6 months.

Oh, my, I would have to post pone our wedding. I knew Reiny would not like that. What was I to do?

When I told Reiny he held me and said,

"Please, sweetheart, wait until after we are married to have the operation, so I can take care of you, day and night. You'll need someone at night and you won't let me do it before the wedding."

What a thoughtful man. No wonder I loved him.

I could hardly walk. Would I have to go down the aisle in a wheel chair? Everyone would really feel sorry for Reiny then!

I went back to the surgeon and told her what Reiny wanted. She set me up with a pain clinic that would get me thru the wedding and the honeymoon, but then I would have to have the operation. Oh, I was so excited. Was it possible for me to be without pain? That just seemed too good to be true.

A New Car

I still worked out on the NuStep equipment every day. Reiny would ride the bicycle right next to me and we could talk. He said he did it because he didn't want anyone to work out next to me. I began to realize he was not feeling secure in my love.

After supper each night Reiny would come over and we would watch our favorite programs. He liked to watch Lawrence Welk and that was one of my favorite shows too. He knew him personally and had gone to his dances in the Dakotas. I am feeling more comfortable with Reiny all the time. He is such a good cuddler.

Reiny took me and his local family out to a nice restaurant on a golf course, to celebrate his oldest daughter, Vicki's birthday. The food was good and the fellowship nice. I like his family and enjoyed the evening. He treats me like a Queen.

Afterwards we watched 'Dancing with the Stars.' It was fun to see which couple got eliminated. We tried to guess which one it would be, but we often guessed wrong. Reiny would say,

"Why did they eliminate them? That other couple was a lot worse than they were."

It made him a little mad. He also felt the girls ought to wear more clothes. As he didn't leave until 10:30; Mother said,

"Reiny is coming earlier and leaving later all the time."

Of course that was true because we found it easy to talk with one another, and enjoy each other's company. So why not?

The Lord seemed oh so close today. I put on my pretty pink suit before breakfast, because I was going out to the next town north, Keizer, and speak at the 'Christian Woman's Fellowship' meeting. My talk seemed to go over really well.

That night I was exhausted when Reiny came over to watch the Seattle Mariners play on T V. We always bet on who will win. I just take whichever side he doesn't. The loser has to take the other one out to dinner. The winner gets to pick the restaurant. What fun. We yell and root for our team of the evening. It turns out to be a lovely evening. I keep track of who wins and write it down in my journal. No cheating is possible. As Reiny left he said,

"Sweetheart, let's go car shopping tomorrow."

That kind of surprised me, but I was happy as his car had 'dog' smell in it. I guess a man never gets too old to want a new car. We had given up looking for Motor Homes, for now anyway. I was glad.

He picked me up before breakfast and we ate Hawaiian French toast on the way to a Toyota dealer in McMinnville. I was told you could always get the best deal in McMinnville. He got lost getting there but we enjoyed each other's company so I didn't care. He finally did stop and asked for directions to the Toyota dealer. I thought that was a real plus point for him as most men just hate to stop and ask for directions.

We found a new Scion XD in silver, four doors, with a stick shift. It got 40 miles to the gallon and only cost $15,000. It was towable just as it came, that was a plus. Reiny still thought he would like to tow a car behind a motor home. They also had a hybrid but it wasn't towable and cost $29,000. I really didn't think we would ever buy a Motor Home but apparently he did.

"Let's look in Salem, tomorrow, honey. We can always come back if this proves to be the best deal" I whispered in Reiny's ear.

Sure enough, the next day we went to a Toyota dealer in Salem and signed for a silver Scion, stick shift, towable. It was real cute.

As we traded in his car he drove the new car home. I saw him jerking, stopping, and starting it. I was glad

I was not in it. When we got to our homes he leaned out his window and motioned me over to our new car,

"Hop in and I'll take you to Kentucky Fry's for supper."

Reluctantly I jumped in the car and fastened my seat belt. I noticed he revved up the motor as his foot was so big and heavy. It just didn't fit on the little peddle. For the most part he was a good driver and I felt safe with him, but this was beginning to scare me. Then we started up the hill by where we lived.

"Help, help! My poor neck!" Either he never knew how to drive a stick shift, or had forgotten. This car was just too little for him and tested his coordination beyond its limits.

The next day we took the new car to church. Oh my, oh my!

This was just not working with Reiny and the stick shift. The next day I drove the little thing up to Portland to the V A hospital. It was not a problem. I did really well. *Reiny just cannot do a stick shift with his big feet. We might have to think about another option*, I thought. One losses so much money when you first drive off the dealers lot, that we neither one wanted to even think about it, but Reiny driving the little car just wasn't going to work.

My back pain, meanwhile, was getting worse and worse. Reiny had such a fun sense of humor it took my mind off of my pain most of the time. He was so patient with me when I walked "funny".

Finally I gave in and took a pain pill. I felt sick all day. I was like a rag doll. Reiny really made me laugh when he left that night, after watching T V. He put his hands through his hair and really messed it up, then pulled his shirt part way out and turned on my porch light.

"What are you doing?"

"All those old women watching out their windows will see me and wonder what's been going on in here." He grinned.

He is so funny and cute, I thought.

Buddy

Reiny had put an ad in the local paper to give away his dog. So one day, during lunch, a lady and her kids came to take Reiny's dog, "Buddy," away. When I came out of the' big house' to go home I saw the lady backing out and hurried to Reiny. He was crying. He loved his little doggie so much.

"I love Buddy, but I love you more."

He whispered in my ear as I reached for him to hold him. Everyone told him he should have given me up and kept the dog. I'm glad he didn't. I would take him over to see Buddy in his new home many times. Reiny would bring him treats and stay and pet him but only for five minutes or so and then Reiny was ready to go home.

When Reiny got back in the car he would always assure himself how happy Buddy was with the children, and how good they were to him. They took pictures of Buddy and sent them to us on the internet. Reiny really appreciated that.

While watching T V that night I told Reiny about my plans for his birthday that was coming up. I hoped that would help get his mind of his dog, Buddy. He seemed very pleased. He was not a 'jump up and down' person like I was, but I got so I thought I could read him pretty well.

He always hated to go home at night. *It will be so nice when we are married, I thought. I love him so much.*

Reiny's grandson, Josh, helped deliver our new double recliner. This will be nice. We both enjoy a recliner and this will be nice for cuddling too.

The double recliner was fun for cuddling but one evening as we were playing in it, Reiny decided to exit over the side and it tipped over with us in it. There we were under the recliner both laughing so hard neither one of us could push the thing off of us. It took us awhile to stop laughing long enough to get the big recliner off of us. Then we had to get ourselves up. We were a bit more careful after that.

Reiny's 88th Birthday

My youngest son, Michael, had arrived with his son, Ivan. They always got me a mocha at Star Bucks before breakfast. They stayed in the guest room at 'the big house.' Ivan had been adopted from Russia and was such a handsome lad. He was so nice you couldn't help but love him. He had grown almost as tall as I was. He was only 12 years old, as best anyone could figure.

Michael and Ivan came down in a beautiful yellow, mustang convertible. It was fun to ride in. Reiny's birthday was coming up and as he loved the Seattle Mariners, Mike helped me get tickets to a ball game in Seattle, via the internet. We also secured a room at a motel near by the park. This was going to be fun.

A friend, Bonnie, gave me her meal tickets to pay for Mike and Ivan's meals. That was so thoughtful. She is the sweetest woman, a real southern belle.

I hated to see Mike and Ivan leave as it would be a long time, I knew, before I would see Ivan again.

The next day I heard the front door rattle and looked at the clock. It was only 5:45 a. m. I stumbled out of bed, threw my robe around me and headed for the front door, not in the best of moods at that early hour. Reiny brought in the coffee, took one look at me and quickly left. Good idea. I didn't even wish him a Happy Birthday!

At 9:00 I picked Reiny up and we drove to Seattle, stopping at 'Spiffy's" to split a pecan roll and have a cup of coffee. We made it to the motel at exit 134 by 12:30. Not bad timing. We slept until Mike picked us up at 4:30 for the ball game. My sciatic nerve made it hard to walk.

Mike was able to drop us off right in front of our gate. They were giving away Bobble heads of

Ishiro, our favorite player. We each got one. We took the elevator to the 1st floor and our seats were not far from the elevator. After Mike parked the car and came up, he became our arms and legs. That was so helpful. He bought Reiny a hooded jacket for me to give to him for his birthday. As the wind had come up he needed it to keep warm.

Even though the game was very good, because of the chilly wind we left at the seventh inning. We watched the rest of the game from our nice warm motel room.

The next day after breakfast we decided that we were too tired to do the museum scene, or any other scene. We just headed home. Reiny drove all the way home, I semi dozed all the way.

We made it home for lunch, and then both took a nap. This traveling was wearing us out. I was so glad we hadn't bought that motor home. We were just too old, and got worn out too fast, to enjoy traveling like we both used to.

It snowed off and on all the next day. This seemed a little late in the year for snow. *I hope Reiny doesn't take the car out in this. I'm sure we're going to have to trade it in on another. I thought.* We were trying to make the little car work for us but it just wasn't going to work.

After church at Turner, we went back to the Toyota dealer to see what we could do. We traded it in on a blue car with an automatic shift. The new car didn't have a cruise control so we left it, and had it added.

"Now, we won't be able to pull it with a Motor Home," Reiny lamented. I doubted if he and I would go Motor Homing anyway. I was happy because now we had a blue car, my favorite color for a car.

Though we were tired, we did go to the Turner church that evening. I wanted Reiny to get to know some of the people in the church we would attend. He came over to the house afterwards and we talked while enjoying the comfort of the double recliner. I was finding out way more than I wanted to know about his past. He said,

"I wish I had met you when you were single in the 70's." he told me.

"I don't think I would have given you a second glance, except that you were so good looking." I informed him.

He was so tired from the week-end he fell asleep in the recliner, then got up and sleepily staggered home at 9:00. I was concerned about him.

The next day Reiny brought coffee over at 6:45 a.m. He stayed this time and drank with me. We drove out to the Western Shop and got him a leather vest. He had wanted one, he said. I knew that as he had told me several times. He looked very good in it too.

Ginny, my dear friend, volunteers at the senior center yearly rummage sale. She called me on the cell phone to let me know there was a king size bed for sale. She knew Reiny and I were looking for one. We dashed down to the senior center and bought it. My grandson, Dan, volunteered to deliver it the next day, so they put a sold sign on it for us.

The next day when he came to pick it up, he found it wouldn't fit in his truck. His truck had its canopy on. Another man at the center was able to get it in his truck and with Dan's help delivered it and put it together for us.

Now we had to buy a mattress. We would put my bed into our spare bedroom and Reiny had promised to give his bed to one of his grandkids.

We ate on the patio of Reiny's oldest daughter, Vicki, and her husband, Maur. They have such a beautiful back yard. Then Maur drove us all to Portland to an Eastern Orthodox Church. There we watched all ages do Greek dances.

Reiny sat in the front seat and I sat in the back with Vicki. We had a nice talk. She thinks of me more as a sister than a step mother. It doesn't really matter to me. Whatever she is comfortable with is fine with me.

Before I went home that night Reiny ask if I'd go with him to his grandson's place in Washington, where he stored his Motor home. Of course, I would.

Reiny picked me up after breakfast and we drove up to his grandson, Mark's, place in White Salmon, Washington. Reiny had stored his motor home there and wanted Mark, his grandson, to sell it for him, if possible. We were bringing up the title. Only problem was his daughter's name was on it too and he hadn't gotten her to sign it, so we took the title back with us. It turned out to be a lovely trip anyway.

As a treat Reiny took me to dinner at a motel, on the river, in Hood River. We split a yummy, sea food dinner, and still couldn't eat it all. We watched tug boats, and a speed boat, traveling on the river. It was a very pleasant evening and very romantic.

The only fault I could think of in Reiny was that his family kept telling me he was tight with his money. I looked for signs of this but never found any. He was always very generous with me. If I wanted to donate to a charity or a missionary cause, he would always match whatever I gave. I had to be careful what I told him I liked, as he would want to get it for me.

We went over to the Turner church today. Reiny is beginning to know people and really likes some of them. He always gives my mother a hug and kiss. She seems to appreciate that.

My son Tom called and they have their plane tickets to come to the wedding. It is just May and we don't get married until July but I guess you need to get the tickets ahead of time to get a good deal.

Becoming a Family

We are becoming a family with family problems. Reiny's great granddaughter is graduating from High School in Roseburg, the same night as my granddaughter, Taylor, has her dance recital. As we are going to Reiny's great grandson, Noah's, violin concert, we'll go to Taylor's dance. Whee! Already it is starting and we haven't even gotten married yet.

Mike is in Florida at a new job. Now I have a son in each time zone. In spite of that, they are so good to come help me whenever I need it. I am so grateful.

We got our proofs of the wedding invitations. I like them. They have a nice picture that Mike took while he was here, of Reiny and me. Reiny's daughter, Tami, will address Reiny's invitations for him. I will need to start mine soon. Time is just whizzing by.

Tonight at supper Reiny and I sat at a table with Tony and Lenore. Reiny told me he loved me in German, Tony said it in Italian, Lenore in German, and I in Spanish. What fun having an international table.

Today was our Christian Woman's Fellowship meeting at my friend Betty Patterson's home. As I walked in the door I saw presents lined up all along the entry way.

Oh, dear, I didn't remember that I was to bring a present for something! I thought.

It turned out I was not to bring a present as this was my first bridal shower. What fun, and what fun gifts I received. I laughed at some measuring spoons that said "a tad, a smidge, and a pinch." Then there was a recipe for Elephant stew. I bet I use that one a lot! Everyone gave me a recipe.

That was sure a good idea as I didn't have any of my recipes any more. I had given them all away. I appreciated their thoughtfulness so much and the cooking things as I didn't have any of those things anymore either.

Betty served strawberries dipped in chocolate and cake. What a nice party. I began to feel like I was indeed getting married again.

When I got home Reiny came over. I showed him our things we got at the shower. He was as delighted as I was with our shower gifts.

"I lost money at the casino, today. I am not going there anymore." He informed me sadly. I was glad.

We went mattress hunting at Woodry's. My lower back was so painful the day was not fun. In spite of that we were able to find the perfect one for us at a price we liked too. They will deliver it. We just have to be there.

Time is Running Out. Are We Ready?

It was time to start the shots for my back pain. I was apprehensive.

Reiny gladly took me to the pain clinic and we learned I would have a series of shots with a certain time between each shot. I figured it up and the last shot would be just a few days before the wedding. That was cutting it awfully close.

"Most people have to wait a long time for their turn to get the series of shots. Are you some kind of celebrity? " The doctor asked me.

"No," I laughed, and I told him my wedding story.

After the first shot I would need someone to stay with me all night, they informed me.

God is good and had brought a friend, Vesta, into my life. She was a nurse. I asked if she would stay all night with me and she readily agreed. Reiny felt much better about the whole procedure. He truly did love me. I was so blessed.

The day of the shot procedure came. I had to lay face down on a table with my head in a hole. They put a huge needle into my back.

This better be worth it, I thought. I had to stay in a room for a while before I could go home, but they let Reiny in with me. When I could go home, they wheeled me out as he drove the car up.

After my friend, Vesta, arrived Reiny went back home but gave instructions to call him if we needed him. Actually Vesta and I had a real good time. We did "girl" talk and giggled and laughed. I slept well. Having Vesta was so nice!

The next day Reiny was over bright and early to check on me and make sure I got my Mocha. He took me out to get corsages for my mother & me for Mother's Day. We got groceries for Mother's Day too. After church on Mother's Day Reiny helped fix a nice meal of prime rib and shrimp. That was my favorite meal. Mother enjoyed it too.

My widow friends from Corvallis always met on a Wednesday at Shari's and I was invited too. I was up by 6:00am and headed down to meet with them and devour a strawberry crepe. I used the opportunity to pass out our wedding invitations. One of my friends had married a few months ago. She said it was so wonderful. Her new husband appreciated everything she did. She highly recommended getting married later in life.

After the get together, my friend, Pat, and I went hunting "pretties" for me. We didn't have any luck. Later on in the week, Tami, (Tim, my oldest son's wife) and I went bridal dress hunting. Reiny and I had already looked close to Salem at the malls and bridal shops but found nothing, except a dress that cost $1,000.

I knew just what I wanted. As one gets older arms become somewhat unattractive, therefore, I wanted a long sleeve jacket, but a see thru one. The wedding would be in July, so white would be acceptable, and I wanted it to hit below the knees, but not be as long as a formal.

Tami had a store in mind at an outlet mall. I met her there. I looked around and found nothing. When a salesclerk came up to us I described what I had in mind. She left us, walked way to the side and end of the store, grabbed a dress, walked back, and handed it to me.

I scooted into the dressing room and tried it on. It was so pretty. I couldn't believe it. The dress was exactly what I had in mind. Now as Tim and Tami were buying it for me I had not looked at the price yet. When I walked out to show Tami she informed me it was on sale and that they had figured to spend more so was there something else I would like?

"Oh, No. I can't believe this. Someone read my mind when they designed this. " I was so happy!

Flu season was upon us and several at the retirement home where we lived were ill. The management declared "a lock down."

"Honey, do you want to go to Shari's with me for dinner, as we are in a lock down?"

Now a lock down means no one can come in and they bring our meals to us. We eat in our rooms.

"Sure, sounds like a good idea. Let's drop off our thirty day notice at the office as we go by."(This was required when one moved.).

It was 86 degrees outside and such a nice day. Reiny and I took advantage of the lovely weather and did a lot of outside errands. There are fewer germs outside too.

We opened a joint banking account. When a couple gets married later in life, finances can really be a problem. Not so much for them but for their grown kids. We decided we would each put $1000 in our joint account each month. Which we faithfully did. Then out of our joint account we would pay, rent, groceries, gas, and any other joint bill we had. Rx's, Dr. co-pays etc. we each paid out of our own account.

We never had a problem with finances. It might have been because Reiny was very generous and often ask me out to dinner and said "I'll pay!" He would put gas in my car. He claimed he paid the rest of his life for not paying for me on our first date. That $3.00 cost him many times over, he claimed. He was right too.

Reiny had a problem calling me my name, Joanne. He would forget and call me his former wife's name, which was similar to mine. In order to break him of this I had him agree to pay me $50.00 every time he forgot and called me her name, by mistake. I could tell he was really trying hard not to forget but he slipped and I told him it made me sad.

I got up and walked over and got his check book and handed it to him.

"Are you serious" he wanted to know?

"You better believe it. It makes me think you are thinking of her, instead of me."

I gave him a pen and he started writing. I spelled my name so he would be sure and spell it right. He laughed and made out the check, signed it and handed it to me. I knew he didn't expect me to take it but I did and said,

"Thank you very much. Now, let's see, what shall I buy with this to make me feel better?"

"You know I love you. I will not ever call you by the wrong name again." I was pretty sure he was right as $50.00 was big enough that he didn't want to lose it very often, and the second time would be $100.

I waited awhile then took out the check, tore it up, and handed him the pieces. He seemed so relieved. He was right; he never did call me by the wrong name again. Isn't it funny how money can help your memory?

One day, Maur, Reiny's son in law, picked him up to take him to see his granddaughter's track meet in a town just southwest of us. The same day, my friend, Elaine, from a town just northeast of us, picked me up, and we went to lunch at the Flight

Deck. Their crab melt is the best in the world and melts in your mouth.

It was good to get away for a while, and just have girl talk. *Maybe Reiny needed to get away too. We are both kind of independent. We'll have to remember not to smother one another*, I thought.

When I got home I wrapped my first book, (I *Swam* With *Piranhas and Still Have my Toes*) to send to Reiny's sister. She was his only other living sibling. He wanted her to read it. She did read it and we have been friends ever since.

Reiny came home in time for us to shop for a table for our new place. We found one that had a long bench with a back. Family gatherings usually end up at my house; the fact that it would seat ten people made it very appealing. It would fit perfectly in the spot we had in mind for it. They will deliver the table after I get moved. We both felt very good about it.

I took a break from packing, shopping and getting ready for the wedding, by traveling to Eugene to attend a Writer's Conference. My arthritis was so bad I could hardly walk. I was blessed when a writer named, Jan, stepped up to help me, and then stayed with me all day. I thought, *what would I do without my wonderful sisters in the Lord?*

When I pulled into my parking spot Reiny came out and got in the car. I'm taking you to Red Lobster for supper and then dancing at the senior center. He was taking me but I was driving. That was O K by me. We laughed and had a lot of fun in spite of my pain. He was so much fun to be with.

It was time for Reiny to meet my granddaughter, Taylor, Tim's and Tami's daughter. We met them at one of my favorite restaurants in Portland. Reiny was very loving and fun. Taylor was so sweet. Reiny and Taylor got along just fine.

When we left, he bent down and gave her a grandpa hug, and told her

"I like little girls"

I told her, "He likes big girls too." He was going to be a nice addition to our family.

Our retirement place was still under lock down the next day, but after Reiny brought over our coffee he ran down to the main building and got me hot chocolate so I could have my Mocha. What a sweetheart he was.

We went to church at Turner again then we joined a group from there that went out to a restaurant to eat every Sunday. It was fun. Reiny fit in so well. We watched a ball game in the afternoon.

Finally the 'Lock Down' was over and we all got to go back to eat in the main dining room. It was fun seeing everyone again. When I moved I knew I would miss everyone, but Reiny said he would cook for our friends and we could invite them all over. That would be fun.

" I think it is time to get our honeymoon reservations, Sweetheart. Let's go today and get it over with. I pay for it, don't I, as you are paying for the wedding?"

"Yes, that's how it usually goes!"

He drove over to the AAA and we sat in front of their travel agent.

"Joanne has never been on the Alaskan Cruise so that's where I'd like to take her."

The agent gave us some brochures. They looked really fun. We would leave right after the wedding and go to Vancouver, Washington. Stay all night, then drive to Bellingham where I wanted to show Reiny my hometown. The next day we would board the ship in Vancouver, Canada, for Alaska. How exciting!

"Yes, that's what we want." Reiny paid and we headed for the car. When we got in the car he said,

"The price doesn't sound so bad if you say it real fast." He told everyone at supper the same thing. *He is so funny,* I thought.

When we told my mother about our honeymoon she said, "Don't break the poor fellow before you even marry him."

The next day we headed over to the Turner Post Office to get our pass ports. Problems, problems,

problems! My driver's license had a typo on the address. I had to order another one and it would take up to five days to get. Reiny's drivers' license was from Washington. We'd have to get him an Oregon I D card. That proved hard too as they demanded mail proof of where he lived. We finally found an insurance policy that was sent to him within the thirty days required. They would accept that. He got his I D card.

"We'll just try again for our pass ports when my driver's license comes in." I reassured him.

I knew this was hard on Reiny as he was a 'DO IT NOW' person and 'wait' was not in his vocabulary. But wait we did. The next week my license came and we did get our pass ports and found our birth certificates. We were ready for the best honeymoon ever.

Because of Reiny's lack of education, he felt timid around all my minister friends. He was very brave and went with me to my Retired Minister's Meeting and luncheon.

He soon felt very accepted and found out preachers were a really fun bunch. We all sang and I heard his voice for the first time. It was soft and mellow like Andy Williams. Oh, I liked it. Life with him was going to be nice.

After church one Sunday Reiny and I watched a memorial Concert from Washington D. C. Reiny cried (sobbed really) as they showed pictures and told about World War 2. His war. He is a very sensitive and loving man.

Born Again Reiny

"Please tell me about getting your sins forgiven and joining the Turner church. I accepted Jesus at a Billy Graham crusade years ago but my last wife wouldn't go to church with me. I offered to go to her church with her but she didn't want to go there either. I really miss it and feel like I want to get right with God. Can you help me?"

I immediately called our pastor, D H, to get an appointment to talk with him. We did and Reiny decided to be baptized in the Turner church. Immersion is our form of baptism, so we showed Reiny scriptures and the meaning of the scriptures on which we based our believe in baptism by immersion.

That night he called his daughter, Vicki, and invited her and her husband to the baptism. He was really excited.

"I want my old friends to know I got my sins washed away and I can say I was born again. I'll be going to heaven." He could hardly wait, but wait he must.

Meanwhile my time to move out of the retirement home and go to our duplex in Turner was fast approaching. Dan (my grandson) came over early one morning and cleaned out a closet and under the bed. He moved it all over to the Turner house. Reiny meanwhile put more slats on our bed frame so the big king size mattress wouldn't sag.

What did *I* do, you wonder? Well, I took pain pills and got dizzy and nauseas. I was lots of help. I was able to plug in my electric scooter but to no avail. It wouldn't take a charge. I might have to take my walker on the honeymoon. I was so glad there was a game on T V in the afternoon so I had an excuse to sit and do nothing but cuddle. There was an upside to my pain.

I got pain pills at Fred Meyers. They made me dizzy, sweaty, nauseas, and didn't work on the pain at all. I just sat around most of the day. A pretty much wasted day for me. I did have a good laugh though when, Sharrie, our activity director, overheard the housekeepers asking me why I liked Reiny, and I told them,

"He has a nice tongue." I meant, of course, that he had a 'silver tongue' and said nice things to me.

She took it the wrong way and teased me. It was funny. I needed a good laugh.

I got another pain medicine. It did nothing. I certainly hope the epidermal shots work out. I cried all day and Reiny was so good about holding me.

Ray, Reiny's son, wants us to pick him up at the airport tomorrow. He wants to buy Reiny's Motor Home and drive it to Spokane.

We were on the road to the airport by 6:30 am. I had no trouble spotting Ray, as he looks like his Dad, only taller and younger, of course. He is very nice looking. On the trip up to the Motor Home he told me about his pretty wife, Sandy, and how he met her, and misses her. He also shared about his childhood. Reiny's past scares me as to how it will affect our future. He seems to want things done 'RIGHT NOW'. That has its good and bad side.

"I believe those blinking lights are telling you to pull over, Honey." I was in the back seat and tapped him lightly on the shoulder.

Reiny pulled over and got out his driver's license.

"Do you know how fast you were going?" the policeman inquired.

Reiny was not happy when he was handed a ticket.

"Don't tell anyone now that I got a speeding ticket."

"In your dreams I won't. I can hardly wait to get back to the retirement home." I teased him. He turned around and gave me a disgusted look. I just smiled and winked at him.

Soon after we got back home I called my sister, Joyce, in Portland. A nurse answered. Joyce's husband, Dale, was taking medicine for his bladder infection and it made him go out of his head. He fell off the toilet and she couldn't get him up.

Then Joyce passed out. They took Dale to the E R for 3 hours, and then admitted him to the hospital. They took Joyce to the E R also. Her blood sugar was 24 and her heart was 34. She wants me to come up and stay with her. She doesn't want to come down here. We'll see when she's ready to come home.

How wonderful! Diane, Joyce's daughter from California, is coming up and will care for her mom.

The day had finally arrived for Reiny's baptism. Vicki and Maur pulled into the parking lot of the Turner Christian church as Reiny and I were getting Mother out of the car. Reiny was so excited as he followed the pastor to the front of the church and back to the dressing room for his baptism. It was to be a family only affair. Our new neighbor, Jerry, was also a minister at the church and he gave the prayer. The minister, D H said a few words to Reiny and then leaned him back into the water and pulled him up.

Reiny later said he felt "years of sin roll off me." From that moment on he tried to say and do what he felt a Christian should do. He didn't want to be a hypocrite as he felt some of his friends had been. God had given me a good man indeed!

From that day on he always had devotions with me either before or after breakfast. He led prayer before we ate, even if we had company or we were out in public. We often read the Bible sometime during the day and had our prayers together before bed.

After we were married I often got up and played hymns on the piano and sang first thing in the morning. He would come out and stand behind me and sing, while lovingly putting his hands on my shoulders. He said he remembered his parents singing hymns in their parlor. It was a nice memory he had. He made a good memory for me also.

How blessed we were that our new neighbor at Turner was the wife of one of the minister's at the church where we were worshiping. She was multi-talented and made our beautiful wedding cake that served 150 people. We were so pleased. We had rented a fountain for sparkling cider. My favorite bubbly. I used that drink a lot on holidays and it would be fun at the wedding. (It was too)

After I had moved, my dear friend, Erlaine, met me for lunch. That was so nice I didn't have to fix something to eat and eat it all alone. She gave me a wedding gift and she let me open it. Ooooh how nice! It was a nightie and matching robe. My friends wanted me to look nice for Reiny.

The next day I had so many things to do on my list but my back was hurting too much. My son, Tim, called and gave me some exercises to do and they did seem to help. I was able to get a lot done.

5 Weeks Left Is All

I woke up to the phone ringing.

"Happy Birthday, honey! I'll be over and take you out soon."

"Better wait for a little while. It is still pretty early, but thank you for calling. You are the first to wish me Happy Birthday."

With that he began to sing Happy Birthday to me. That was so sweet. A little over a month and I would be this man's wife. Soon after I was up and dressed the doorbell rang. There stood the florist with a dozen long stemmed red roses in a pretty vase. They were just beautiful and even smelled good.

The card on the roses said, "I love you." No need to sign your name to that. The arrangement was 28 inches high. When Reiny came over and saw the roses he seemed so proud of himself and rightly so. He should have been.

That night Reiny took me out to "Newport Grill" for prawns, and handed me another gift in a small beautifully wrapped box. Wow! What a man!

"You are spoiling me, and I love it."

He just grinned. I opened the little box and there was a pair of sparkling Emerald earrings. I put them on immediately so he could admire them too, then leaned over the booth and kissed him a thank you, very quickly as I knew he would not let me get away if I didn't catch him by surprise. I didn't want to make a scene. I would kiss him properly when we got home or back in the car. (or both) What a birthday! Life with Reiny was going to be something else.

Just 2 Weeks Until The Wedding

Reiny and I went to the Turner Church and when the invitation was given to come forward and join the church we walked down the aisle and joined.

After church we drove to Portland to watch granddaughter Taylor's dance performance. It was excellent and we both enjoyed it. What a fun day!

All week long we did wedding errands. I find it hard to get used to Reiny's 'DO IT NOW!' attitude.

I'm learning to work around it though. Everyone has a flip side.

The cable man set us up with cable and internet today at our new house. With Reiny's nice T V and mine also, we'll have one in the living room and one in our bedroom too. I thought that would be nice if we each wanted to watch something different. But NO! The first time I went into the bedroom to watch a favorite program of mine that he didn't like, I found out that it wasn't going to work. I was really into my program when I heard this moaning, forlorn cry from the front room.

"Where is my wife? I miss her. I am all alone out here."

Before I could answer, (I was laughing), he plopped himself down on the bed and said, "What are _we_ watching?" That ended our separateness.

I picked up my Harp very carefully and carried it out to the car. It had a cover over it as I didn't want it to get scratched. It was hard to squeeze it into the back seat, but I made it. I never let movers move it for me. They could take the piano but not my Harp. It looked heavy but actually my kind of harp is hollow and light as a feather, just awkward to handle. I drove carefully and we made it just fine. I would have to tune it again and that was quite a job but I didn't mind.

In the afternoon Reiny came over and we watched a Mariners game. We always bet on who would win. The loser had to pay for a shrimp dinner at McGrath's. I had to pay this time.

Today Reiny and I went to the grocery store and bought our first groceries together, out of our joint account. We spent $184.29 and I forgot the onions. We put the groceries away and now all we need is to get married and we can start playing house. Reiny moans and groans when it's time for him to go home at night. It is just 2 weeks until the wedding. I try to encourage him with,

"It won't be long now, honey. Then you can stay all night."

Pat, my friend from Corvallis, drove up and brought me some 'pretties'. We ate lunch at Aumsville, a town just a short distance away. We had lots of laughs and lots of fun. She helped me get my computer up and going too. After she left Reiny came over and we were going to unpack some boxes but we discovered we were both too tired. We just settled in and watched T V. instead. You may find as you get old, it is hard to tell 'being lazy' from old age symptoms.

The next Sunday when I saw Reiny's car come up the driveway I went on out to meet him. That way he didn't have to get out of the car. He drove to church and afterwards over to his youngest daughter, Tami's, for a lovely chicken dinner she had fixed for us, to celebrate Father's Day. Her son, Josh, spent the afternoon hanging our drapes in our new place. Josh would prove to be so much help in the year ahead.

This moving was really getting strung out and I was getting very weary. (Old age, not laziness, I'm sure.) After I took Reiny to get an eye exam, I dropped him off at his place. I was picking up the granddaughter, Sarah, of one of my friends, to help me unpack. She proved to be a real help and did an exceptionally good job of unpacking and putting things away. After I took her home I found two more boxes that we had missed, but as I wasn't lazy, just old, I was able to tackle them later on.

On my way back from taking Sarah home I picked up Reiny and we went out for fish again. Eating out with him was so much fun and I always learned so much about him.

Our new neighbors, two doors down, invited us to their house, along with several of our other neighbors, to get acquainted, and have dessert. I was worried for Reiny as I knew he had trouble hearing and was worried. The hostess sat next to him and she spoke loud enough for him to hear easily. They hit it off right away. All of the new neighbors up on the hill where we would be living went to the same church that we did. They were all

very nice and friendly.

Just a few days left

"What did I do? The T V won't work at all. I can't get any channels" Reiny was frustrated and with good reason.

I called 'help' and they said they would put in an order to come check it out tomorrow. Next we called grandson, Josh, and he said,

"Put it back on '3', grandpa." We did and it worked great. Sometimes we just need a little help from the younger generation.

We found out our neighbors are called 'The Hill Toppers" as we live on the hills in Turner. The Hill Toppers invited us to eat with them at a buffet. The couple two doors down invited Reiny and me to ride with them. It was fun getting acquainted. They were so nice and Reiny felt very much at ease with them. He told me he could tell they lived their faith and didn't just talk about it. That meant a lot to him.

I was so glad he was feeling at home even before he moved in. Most of his stuff was already moved over and in a few days he could start living there too.

Meanwhile we went to celebrate Father's Day again, courtesy of Reiny's oldest daughter, Vicki, and her husband. They were in Washington D. C. so had given a gift card to him. We went to one of our favorite places and watched the airplanes come and go while we ate. He again got some good shrimp and was a happy 'Father'.

"I'd like the Zoller family castle picture to go over the fireplace, please." I instructed grandson, Josh.

Josh and his family had come over to put up our pictures. They were just too heavy for Reiny and me, especially his ancestor's German castle picture. We had it reframed with non-glare class. It was one of my favorite pictures.

I fixed us all German sausage and beans for lunch. Reiny seems to like everything I cook, except he doesn't like vegetables, no matter who cooks them. After we were married I had to sneak them in casseroles or something else he really liked.

"Drive the car into the garage, but don't run me over. Stop! That's just where I'll put the string."

Reiny was marking where I needed to stop the car in the garage so I wouldn't hit the hot water tank. That was so thoughtful of him. It worked, too, as neither of us ever hit the hot water tank. If we came in just right there was room for my electric scooter as well.

After I had moved into our new house Reiny wanted to come over to Turner every day, and he did. He built shelves for his tools in the garage and put up his family pictures right above the shelves.

"Honey, you can put those pictures in the house. You don't have to have them in the garage."

"Oh, no, I want them out here. I will be out here a lot and can see them and they will keep me company. " He did love his family, so that is where his family pictures stayed except for a few by his side of the bed. I enjoyed looking at them too

Crunch Time

"Which building is the court house? Where do we park?"

We did found it and Reiny paid the $60.00 for the marriage license. It was good for 60 days only. That made me laugh, a dollar a day. We finally had the 'piece of paper' that Reiny was looking for. He was so happy.

I had to finish getting my back shots. It took three hours this time. When we got back, Reiny put ice packs on me then heated up left over spaghetti for supper. We watched the Mariners again and bet as usual. Afterwards we discovered he had won once and I had won once. He said that made us even. I said, No, we both have to pay. Neither of us really cared.

We took my ring in to get the engagement one soldered to the wedding one. I will miss my ring but it isn't much longer now.

My back pain continues. Those shots better work or I won't be able to go down the aisle.

I couldn't go to church today as the pain was too severe. We watched 'Hour of Power' and it was good. We ate left over salmon sandwiches and

I made banana, peanut butter pudding. He ate 3 bowls full. I think he liked it.

Our two wedding preachers, Tom and Maur, called. They wanted to know how we wanted the service to go. We didn't care. They could divide it up anyway they wanted. We said we would just explain on the program, who was who, what the songs were, and leave the rest up to them to decide who did what, when. They worked it out so nicely.

Reiny and I had a fun day and teased each other a lot. We should both sleep well tonight. He left by 8:30.

"May we open it now?" I ask our friend Ginny. She has just given us 2 beautiful packages.

"Please do."

"What perfect gifts"

We didn't have any placemats and she had given us some very pretty ones. I didn't have any tablecloth to fit our long table, so placemats were just what we needed. The other package was a swivel stool. I would use that a lot every time I was in the kitchen, as I couldn't stand very long with my back ache.

Reiny spent the afternoon happily putting the stool together. We watched another ball game and I won the ball game bet, this time. If you're getting the idea that I'm using theses ball games to sit and rest, wellllllllll you just might be right.

Last Minute Chores

"We should have just let Maur marry us. It would have saved us a lot of money." I lamented as we headed to the car after purchasing cups, plates and ordering napkins, and balloons.

"I can live with it." Reiny smiled. That was his favorite saying. He used it a lot. He used it again that evening when we just had cheese and crackers for supper, because I had just gotten another shot in my back.

"I'm not as dizzy this time, so if you're tired go ahead and go on home. I promise to call you if I need you" He did but I didn't need to call him as he called me several times. I did get along just fine.

The next day I had no pain. I was so excited that I could walk. I had not walked correctly for a long time. Due to pain, I walked a little 'funny'. Reiny said I was his *ducky*, because I waddled. I could tell he was just as happy as I was that I had no pain.

Reiny came over and picked me up to go to a barbeque at the retirement center. We had such fun and laughed a lot. On the way over he stopped at a coffee drive thru and got me a latte. When he handed it to me he smiled and said,

"See, I'm not as tight with my money as they say I am!"

He was right. On the way back to Turner he stopped and got gas. It was $4.18 a gallon. He was using a lot of gas coming and going to and from Turner. Good thing the wedding was not very far off.

"Mom, we're in Portland and will be down tomorrow." My son, Tom and his wife, Janine, their 2 girls, Crystal and Cayla, had arrived from Colorado. They would spend the night at his big brother Tim's and wife Tami's house in Portland, then drive down to Turner in the morning for breakfast. I was very excited.

Bright and early the next day we all met at my mother's place and drove to the next town, Aumsville, for breakfast. I ordered Swedish pancakes. As I could only eat one pancake my granddaughters finished the rest. Reiny fit right in with my family and they loved him right away. Someone took a picture of Reiny and the girls. One of the girls leaned her head on his shoulder. Later when we got the picture he noticed this right away and said,

"My new granddaughters like me. Look at that!"

He seemed to feel accepted. That made me very happy.

"Joanne, your son, Tom has his PHD and I just went to the 8th grade, but he treats me like his equal. How can he do that?"

"Well, of course, honey," I reassured him. "We're all God's children. Some of us just sat in classes longer and read more books, and wrote more papers than others. That doesn't make us any better than anyone else. God wants us to LOVE one another and you and Tom both do a mighty good job of that!"

The next few days before the wedding just flew by. Programs were made on the computer and printed off. Final orders of flowers were given and rose petals were bought for Taylor to sprinkle down the path in front of me. My friend, Allison, from church, gave us a cute fish bowl to put our colored sand in. We had bought pink sand for me to pour into the bowl and blue for Reiny to pour in. This was to demonstrate the blending of our two lives and the pretty design it would make. It worked so nicely but after the service a little child ran up to the fish bowl and started stirring it all up with his hand. Luckily, he only messed up one side of the fish bowl before he was caught and stopped. The other side still had a pretty design. (And does to this day) We had decided that the lighting of a mutual candle wouldn't work so well due to the possibility of wind, as we were going to be outdoors. This was indeed going to be a special wedding. This is what Reiny wanted this time, he said.

"I've only had Justice of the Peace weddings before. I want this one to be very special because you are very special to me." How could I argue with that?

As we were running our last minute errands, we ran into some roadblocks, due to a car wreck, and had to take some detours. Reiny took it well. I called my mother and told her,

"Reiny impresses me more each day and I seem to be falling in love with him more and more each day."

Mother seemed pleased. She liked Reiny.

That night Reiny soaked his feet in a hot vibrator pan that he had, and I fixed hot dogs for supper. He yelled out to me from the living room,

"You look so natural in the kitchen, like you belong there."

"Oh, no, I think it's too late for *'barefoot and pregnant in the kitchen."* We both laughed.

Reiny read the words to the songs that Mike was going to sing at the wedding and shed tears. He has a soft heart. I like that.

All Reiny's furniture was in our new place now and it all fit, (sort of). Not an inch to spare anywhere. We had wall to wall furniture, but who cared. I was beyond trying to impress people. If we could, as Reiny says, "live with it" then it was O K.

As Reiny had moved all his furniture out of his old place; he needed to find a place to sleep. There is a guest room above the dining area at the Turner retirement home so Reiny planned to sleep there. He was not happy with that arrangement as the bathroom was down the hall and there were ladies staying in another guest room there.

"I have to get dressed to go down the hall to the bathroom. Even in the middle of the night. I don't like that."

The next day at 4:30 am Reiny rang the doorbell and said he couldn't sleep as it was too hot and no air conditioning in his room. He came in and showered and shaved. I got up, fixed coffee and had my devotions. Reiny snuck back in the bedroom and fell asleep in our new bed. Tom went down the hall and saw Reiny sleeping in the bed, and then walked to the kitchen where I was,

"Mom, Janine and I are sleeping here. Why don't you let Reiny sleep on the davenport tonight? He needs a good night's rest. It will be OK. No one will talk. Your witness will not be compromised."

So that's what we did and he got a good night's sleep the night before the wedding. He needed it as we had just completed the rehearsal dinner and the rehearsal in the Gazebo. All went very well.

Everyone made it such fun. My family had fun meeting his family. This was going to be a nice match. His family was so nice and accepting of me and my family. We ate in a little room at one of our favorite restaurants in town, and had a lot of laughs. "The Groom" paid the bill, as is the custom. Not a bit of fuss over it either. He was indeed generous.

The Wedding Day

As I started to write in my journal this is what I wrote; *'This day was a blur but I'll try to remember the high lights.'*

The minute my mind realized I was no longer sleeping, even before I opened my eyes, I began talking with my heavenly father about this very special day. It was not hard hopping out of bed even though it was only 3:00 am. I wanted to beat everyone else to the one bathroom. I peeked out of the window to check on the weather. Oh good, no rain today, but it was going to be hot. What did I expect in July?

I quickly made my famous cinnamon biscuits and scrambled eggs for Reiny. The smells from the kitchen woke the others. Soon our household was abuzz.

Tom, Janine, and Angie, assistant administrator of the Turner Homes, started to decorate the Gazebo early before the heat became too bad. When they finished, it was beautiful. They also discovered I had forgotten cream and sugar for the guest's coffee. They took care of that for us old forgetful people.

Tom and Janine helped set up the chairs and were there when the beautiful cake was delivered and the flowers. The guest book was set up and people started coming. My sister and I met in mother's room as planned and I dressed for the wedding.

All of a sudden I saw a commotion up front by the entrance to the gazebo. I strained to see what was going on. All I could see was a big shot gun in the hands of a big man. What was going on?

I wanted to run down and see but I couldn't run down the aisle in my wedding dress. Where were Reiny and our ministers?

Then I caught sight of Tom, Maur, some grand-kids and Reiny. They were all almost doubled over laughing. It seems our neighbor had decided to make this a shot gun wedding. 88 year old Reiny really thought that was great. I don't think the humor was lost on anyone. Reiny probably thought that was the best part of the whole wedding. It made him look like 'Macho Man'. Later, on our honeymoon, when anyone ask him about our wedding, that was the first thing he told them.

My friend, Allison, started to play the electric piano right on time. We didn't want to keep our friends out in the sun any longer than necessary. It was hot!

My handsome eldest son, Tim, tucked my arm in his and we headed down the cement path filled with the rose petals that pretty Taylor was scattering in front of us. As we turned the corner and headed down the final path I was so relieved to hear the 'Wedding March' being played. Allison had told me that she was going to play "The Stripper" music, instead of the wedding march, as I headed down the aisle. I thought she was joking, but one never knows. If she had played it we would all have been doubled over in laughter and the wedding would have been delayed till we could catch our breath.

Tim, when asked,

"Who gives this woman to be married to this man?" answered,

"My brothers and I do." My boys had decided on that answer. It surprised and pleased me.

Tim helped me up on my stool and Reiny got on his stool before Tom started to talk. Tom was tall, dark and handsome, like his daddy and I was very blessed that he was one of the ministers marrying us. Afterwards, Reiny said,

"Tom looked right at me when he gave his talk about marriage and I heard every word."

I was so pleased because Reiny was afraid he would embarrass himself by not being able to hear. It helped him to relax.

How I got three good looking boys, I don't know, but I'm sure it's not just a proud mother talking.

My youngest son, Michael, was a tall blond, Scandinavian. He stepped up and began to sing to Reiny and me. The words were printed in the programs so everyone could follow along. Later Reiny again said,

"Michael sang right to me. He has such a beautiful voice! Do you think he was trying to tell me something?"

Reiny was taking this all so seriously. I was afraid his blood pressure would go up too high so when he looked at me, I winked at him. That made him smile.

Reiny's good looking son in law, Maur, (we only used good looking fellows), finished up the last part of the wedding. We exchanged vows, and slipped our rings on each other, easily. (I had sprayed Windex on my finger so the rings would slip on easily. It worked great.)

I reached back to my sister to get my bridal bouquet and she started to walk forward to hand it to me but she stumbled. Before you could blink an eye, Andy,' the good looking' best man, ran over and caught her. He was certainly attentive and alert.

Maur was about to pronounce us husband and wife and I was getting worried. Reiny had told me earlier,

"I know when we kiss at the end you are going to want to pull away so as not to make a scene, but I'm not going to let you. "

When Maur said " You may kiss the bride," Reiny grabbed both my hands and pulled me close, bent down to kiss me then put his big hand behind my head, so I couldn't get away. I was trapped. To tease me he stuck his tongue in my mouth. Big mistake! I started to bite his tongue gently but my upper teeth fell down and bit him. This surprised him and he let me go, but not before we both got the giggles. We tried to stop laughing and just smile, but my shoulders kept shaking and gave me away. I was so glad to walk back down the aisle on my fun loving husband's arm.

The reception was just a few short steps away. We behaved ourselves when feeding each other the cake. My daughter in law, Janine, had told me before the ceremony,

"You're not going to smash each other in the face with the cake, are you?" Now I have no idea why she would think such a thing.

We were supposed to entwine our arms and feed each other the sparkling cider, but in the excitement of the moment, we forgot. That was probably a good thing as my dress was white and the sparkly drink was red. The two might have met. I'm sure the entwining of the arms would have done it. It did leave me thirsty though.

They gave us chairs to sit on while we greeted everyone. The retirement center where we met and courted brought a bus full of our friends. Reiny had friends and relatives from Washington State, and I had friends from Corvallis and Springfield. We each had friends and relatives from all over Oregon. There was quite a crowd. I was glad for a chair to sit on as the line to greet us was long. After we hugged the last friend we hurried up to our new house, changed clothes, and headed north. We shared the driving.

We were grateful that our kids would help clean up afterwards and carry our gifts to the house. What a job! Reiny's eldest daughter, Vicki, invited the family to their house for supper and to get to know each other better. My kids went and told me afterwards how nice it was. They did enjoy the fellowship and the food.

The Honeymoon

In Vancouver, Washington, Reiny pulled into our motel, unpacked our suitcases, as I checked in. Then we were off to get a bowl of soup. Reiny knew Vancouver very well. He had lived there for years, so he picked the restaurant.

Back in the motel we got ready to spend the first night as husband and wife. He gave a big wolf whistle when he saw me in the sexy nighty my lady friends had given me. That was worth the price of the wedding right there. (He thought so too)

At 3:00 a.m. the alarm radio in our motel room went off. I thought it was a car alarm outside our window. We finally woke up enough to figure it out and got it shut off. It was a little unnerving.

Due to our hectic wedding day and the middle of the night alarm, I felt we probably would both sleep in, but no.

After an early breakfast Reiny took me to see the house he used to live in, then drove around the area and showed me some other things that meant a lot to him. He drove part way up toward Seattle then I finished driving for the day.

"Oh this is such a nice view of the harbor. I'm glad Lenore, (one of our table mates at the retirement center,) recommended it to us. I bet the food is good too." I sighed.

We had stopped at a restaurant on the bay in Fife, Washington. After enjoying crab cocktail and sea food fettuccini, Reiny said happily,

"That nice meal only cost $100.39. It was worth it."

I was shocked, both at the price and my new husband's attitude. We stopped in time to be in bed by 8:00 p.m. We were tired. We both agreed our first day of marriage was lovely!

The next day I drove to Everett, Washington, where we stopped and had pie and coffee at a famous restaurant there. From there it didn't take much longer to make it to Bellingham. This was my old stomping grounds. I knew my way around. After checking into our motel, we ate a good meal on the bay. We were really having fun; just like old people in their second childhood. We watched T V clear up till 10:00. We slept very well.

The next morning we both woke up feeling good. Reiny liked his breakfast in a Greek restaurant right next to the motel. With his tummy full he happily went with me to see where I was raised. My folks had lived in my childhood home for over 60 years. They sold it to a developer when the moved to a retirement home in Oregon. The developer had put several houses on the property. The old original house was still there, but not much else from my childhood was left. The neighborhood wasn't anything like it was when I was a kid living there.

After touring around and showing off some of my favorite spots we ate at a college Pub and eatery. That was fun to see the young people and they seemed amused to see us too. The music wasn't exactly what we were used to but we survived. Reiny could just turn down his hearing aids; I tried to discreetly stuff rolled up napkins in my ears.

After taking a nap at the motel and enjoying getting a back scrub in the shower; we started getting things ready to board the ship the next day.

"Help me find the map to get to the ship. Vancouver, B. C. is not a small town. I will need the map." I pleaded.

After a lot of searching we did find the map.

'Yeah," we will be able to find it now, "I hope".

Sure enough the next day we drove right to the ship, found the place to take our bags and a man ran out and parked our car for us. This was going to be O K.

Lunch on board the ship would not win any prizes and according to Reiny neither would supper. Our room was on the bottom of the ship but right next to the elevator. That was a good thing.

What a surprise awaited us when we opened our cabin door. There on the counter was a beautiful bouquet of flowers (that lasted all week). We had no idea who would have done that. I eagerly reached for the card and it said,

"LET'S CELEBRATE!" It was from Carol, our soon to be daughter-in-law in Florida. The card also included a meal at 'The Pinnacle', a fancy restaurant on board the ship, plus a bottle of Champagne on ice. What a fun way to start our honeymoon!

We were able to sleep o k our first night on the ship and woke early. After a not so good breakfast (Reiny was really disappointed in the food on board) he decided to play in the casino.

I went on deck and made friends with Barb, a nice lady from England. When we talked about my writing, she wanted to buy my first 2 books.

As Barb and I were enjoying visiting on our lounge chairs by the pool, Reiny came walking toward us. As he came close I was going to introduce him to Barb, but he passed me up as if he didn't know me, walked past Barb too without a word. The suddenly reached down, picked up her sandals that were beside her chair, and pretended to throw them in the pool.

"Stop! Stop!" She yelled.

He turned around and grinned as he brought her shoes back.

"Do you ladies want anything to drink? I just won $ 40.00 in the casino."

We both wanted coffee and off he went.

"I'll introduce him when and if he comes back," I laughed.

That night we ate supper with Barb and her husband and their new friends from Australia. Barb told her new friends about my book and they wanted to buy some too. Reiny went down to the cabin and brought a couple books up.

"Now I'll have books in Australia and England. How nice! "

That couple later bought more books to take back with them to give as gifts. I was glad I had put several in my suitcase.

"I believe that makes my books international, what do you think, honey?"

I ask Reiny that night as we were getting ready for bed. He didn't answer. He was hunting a pill for me to take as the boat was tipsy and I was getting nauseas. He found one; I took it and soon drifted off to sleep.

We slept in the following morning as we had had to set our clocks back an hour. Later on in the day we attended a wild life picture show and lecture. It was very interesting.

Lunch proved to keep up their low standards of food. The noodles were not cooked right and were still stiff. Neither one of us ate much but the dessert was excellent, bread pudding and sauce.

"All the waiters are men. Why no women? I like to have some girls and women. Maybe that's why the food isn't good."

Reiny was clearly disappointed.

"The waiters are awfully good about helping us get our plates to our table, and getting anything else we want so we don't have to get up and get it ourselves."

I tried to sooth him. We were having a wonderful time, except for the food.

"The last time I went on this cruise the food was really good." Reiny lamented.

I was a bit embarrassed as Reiny complained to everyone around us. He expresses himself so differently than I do. We seem to have come from two different worlds. Will they collide or run smoothly together, I wondered.

More Honeymoon

The ship loaded at Juneau and many got off. Reiny wanted to stay on board and I didn't mind. That night we found a piano player on the upper deck. We each had a nonalcoholic Peña Colada and relaxed and listened to the great music. Soon a 2 piece band showed up and we danced several dances. It was really nice as he is such a good dancer. This honeymoon was proving to be lots of fun.

We were celebrating our first week of marriage. It was getting better and better every day. We tried to wash our clothes today but there were only two washers. The line to use the washers was very long.

"Sweetheart, just send them out. There is a bag in our room." Reiny generously suggested. We did and got them back the very next day.

We sat by a window and watched the wild life. The otter was so cute and so were the seals playing. Reiny made reservations for our special time at 'The Pinnacle' restaurant.

Wow! Did Reiny ever look sharp! He got all dressed up for our special dinner. With his vest on he looked like Ben Cartwright of Bonanza, with a little bit of Clark Cable thrown in. When I told him that he informed me that he had been mistaken for" him" in his younger days when he had a mustache. I wasn't sure which" him" he was referring to.

The dining experience was a laughing good time. They brought us out some flat seedy bread and olive oil to dip it in. He dipped the bread in the oil and stuck his little finger out as he thought the high society gentleman do.

"I think I ought to ask for a cigar too." He said with a straight face.

When the butter came out in a silver covered bowl, he thought it looked like shaving cream.

We were both having a hard time acting as we knew we were supposed to act. When the hors'douvres came out we did lose it. They brought a big dinner plate with a penny size piece of salmon in the middle with mustard drizzled over it and over the rest of the plate.

We laughed our way through the flaming dinner and then ask for baked Alaska and coffee for dessert. We felt that was appropriate for the occasion.

We were going to go dancing but Reiny had his tennis shoes on. All dressed up with tennis shoes on. We went to the entertainment instead. We both liked it but Reiny said the poor girls didn't have very many clothes on. It was like Las Vegas.

"Oh! This is just like the fjords in Norway." I was so excited. We were passing thru a narrow passage way with snowy mountains and cliffs on either side. The glaciers that we saw were awfully dirty.

"They ought to clean those dirty glaciers for the tourist" I complained.

On Sunday and we went to chapel on board the ship. The room was full and we recognized some of our new friends. After church a couple came up to us and ask to buy my books. They were from New Zealand. God seemed to be using our trip to spread the message he wanted out through my books. I felt very humble and grateful.

When the ship docked at Ketchikan, we stayed on board. We were playing around like teenagers in bed when we heard a key rattle in our door.

"Don't worry, I locked it." Reiny assured me just as the door opened. He threw a sheet over me and faced the surprised steward.

"You better come back later." Reiny greeted him gruffly.

He backed out the door and we began to laugh.

"He probably thought us old folks didn't know how to have fun." Reiny said as he settled back down in bed with a big grin on his face.

"I wonder why he didn't knock. Do you think he was planning on stealing something? He probably thought we were out doing the tourist thing." I was glad we had stayed back on the ship.

We woke early the next day, ate breakfast and were off the ship by 8:15. Found the car, but only after getting some help. We were surprised that the storage for all those days was less than $100.

We only drove as far as Tumwater, Washington. We got a motel and were sleeping soundly by 7:30 p.m. We woke up the next day at 7:30 a.m. We had slept the clock around. I couldn't remember if I had ever done that before. That gave us enough energy to drive all the way home to Turner. We pulled into our driveway just after supper. I didn't even try to unpack. We did muster up enough energy to see what was in the wedding presents and cards. We received lots of gift cards to restaurants so I wouldn't have to cook. Everyone knows as one gets older, planning, grocery shopping, preparing and cooking three meals a day, is a chore. Reiny was aware of this also and he suggested,

"Let's plan on eating one meal a day at a restaurant. We like any of the three meals out. Whichever one of the three meals fits our schedule for that day, we can eat out."

That is just what we did. I never felt tied to the kitchen. Reiny did his share of cooking and was never a slacker when it was time to clean up the kitchen. He either paid out of his pocket, or we took it from our mutual account

We both had extra money at the end of the month as our rent now was just half of what is was over at our retirement home, and we shared the expense. We were each paying less that $400 a month now for rent. Financially marriage was a good idea.

Home Again Home Again Jigady Jig

We unpacked and put suitcases away in the garage. Stocked the kitchen shelves and I planned the next week's menus.

"We've worked pretty hard today. We better take a shower and get our backs scrubbed." Reiny implored.

He knew I enjoyed that so it was an easy sell. The cleaning of the house could just wait for another day. If the house was dirty it assured us we would have company. If it was clean, no one would come see us. It always happens that way.

After the shower, we relaxed and watched Lawrence Welk. He liked this program so much. We just had 'cold cereal' for supper. Reiny was delighted as he picked up his phone to call Ginny, our dear friend, from the retirement home and tell on me. Before I left the retirement home, my table mates had ask me what I was going to feed Reiny for suppers. I had said,

"Oh, cold cereal."

They all felt so sorry for him. Now he was going to tell on me. That was o k as I certainly told on him plenty.

The next Sunday after church, we headed back to our former residence. We had been invited to dinner there. In fact they invited us to come every other week if we wished. (If we wished? Of course we wished.) Their food was always good, especially on Sundays, but best of all was the fun, fellowship, and laughter.

Grandson Josh brought us three discs of wedding pictures and installed them on our computer. We would spend many an hour laughing and reliving our wedding.

Reiny tore up the cardboard boxes from our move and from wedding presents then set them out for the garbage. He used the weed whacker and blower to clean up the outside yard. It looked very nice. I paid bills, and did laundry. We both had just plopped down in the recliner when our doorbell rang.

"You have to tie up your cardboard." The lady next door informed us.

Reiny went out and tried to tie up the cardboard but just couldn't do it. He was discouraged. I called the "shot gun" neighbor and he said he'd take care of it. Reiny was relieved.

We had breakfast at the buffet and it was so good. We shopped at Wal-Mart for granddaughter Anika's baby, and found a cute suit. Found lovely towels for great granddaughter, Summer Dawn's, shower and wedding. Just had to wrap them and we were prepared.

I spent the rest of the day writing thank you notes. By evening I was ready to play. Reiny said,

"Let's go dancing at the senior center."

"I'll be ready in five minutes." I replied on my way to comb my hair and grab my sweater. We had a nice evening. I got him for every dance except the polka and he said he wanted to sit it out and rest.

His former dance partners were getting used to me being there and left him alone.

When we got home we scrubbed each other's backs again in the shower. I always kissed his cute tush, (now some of you may say, butt, I would never say that, of course.) It always made him laugh. We tumbled into bed to cuddle. Marriage is so nice, even at our age.

Our neighbor, Marcia, gave us blueberries. They are plump and look so juicy and sweet, right from her backyard.

"I'll put them in pancakes tomorrow." I told her as I thanked her.

The blueberry pancakes were delicious the next day for breakfast. Our neighbors were so generous to share their produce with us. It made us glad we had moved to Turner.

I hated to leave Reiny, but it was necessary, so I sadly kissed him good-by and drove up to be with my sister in Portland while her husband, Dale, had surgery. The surgery was postponed until 3:30 as they had to pump him full of anti-bionics. When they finally did had the surgery, it went well. We were relieved.

While we were gathering up our coats and things the nurse called again. She said Dale was having trouble breathing. They had to call in two heart doctors to help. We settled back down again to wait once more. Joyce finally got to go in and see him about 7:00p.m. I was exhausted by the time we went to her apartment. We had a nice visit, ate a fruit salad, watched T V and went to bed. I had called Reiny all through the day. He said he was missing me, I was missing him too.

The next day we called the hospital to inquire about Dale, and they said they were sending him home. Joyce would no longer need me so I was able to head to my home and Reiny. When I got in our driveway I called him on my cell phone to come get my suitcase out of the trunk. Boy! Was he happy that I was home! I was happy to be home also.

We did nothing the rest of the day. We seem to be getting awfully good at that.

My old cough just wouldn't go away and seemed to be getting worse. I resorted to Nyquil before bed and didn't cough all night so we both were able to sleep. However when I woke up in the morning I couldn't talk and felt lousy.

In spite of my cold we went to daughter, Vicki's house, to celebrate grandson Andy's birthday. Six great grandkids were there plus the three grown grandkids. The Teriyaki steaks were yummy. They put alcohol in Reiny's coffee because he was catching my cold. It smelled awful. I drove home. Reiny really enjoyed his family and I did too.

I woke up again the next day unable to talk, but Reiny seems to have thrown it off. He cooked breakfast but burnt the bacon and stunk up the place. After we had cleaned up breakfast and before I could clean the house, and before the burnt bacon smell left, the doorbell rang. A woman said,

"I'd like to interview you for the Turner paper."

We invited her in and I opened all the windows to let the burnt bacon smell out. She probably thought it was just the new bride problem. Only this new bride had been cooking before she was born and so had the groom.

The interview went well, the reporter took a picture of us then she was gone. The article in the paper turned out nice as did the picture.

After finally cleaning the house I went to a favorite restaurant and met my longtime friend, Erlaine, for lunch. We split a piece of chocolate cake. That's a good lunch! Reiny ate left over trout at home. I hurried back home to finish the thank you notes. Our friends were so nice. They helped us get started 'playing house' again.

"I think this is the last of the thank you notes. Do you want to stamp them and walk down and put them in the mail box for us?" I ask a relaxing Reiny.

"If you write them, I'll mail them," and he happily did.

We were glad that was done. Reiny barbequed ribs and I baked a potato for supper. My coughing, runny eyes, and nose were getting worse. My head ached and I felt miserable.

It was so nice to curl up together in the double recliner and watch the Olympics. They were being held in China this year. It was fun.

In spite of my misery, the next day we went to the coast. Reiny reserved a motel at Newport Beach for us during his families' "Beverly Beach" reunion that was coming up soon. We drove on up the coast to visit daughter Vicki and Maur's condo. Vicki decorated it so elegantly. While there we watched a wedding on the beach. It was a formal wedding and the bride had on a beautiful long bridal gown but they all were bare footed. Now why didn't we think of that? We could have saved some money on shoes.

We ate at the casino on the beach and Reiny won $40.00 playing Black Jack.

My coughing got worse. I coughed 'till I vomited.

"Honey, I'd give you whiskey for your cough but it really burns."

"No thanks, dear, I'll just use grandma's honey and lemon remedy. That sounds better."

Our friend Ginny was having a birthday.

"I think my cough is somewhat better. I'm not sneezing, and blowing my nose as much as I was. Shall we go over to Ginny's house?"

I did seem to still use a lot of Reiny's hankies. In spite of how I felt we went over to the retirement home to help her celebrate. Probably not a real good idea, but we did it anyway. We were glad we did as it was lots of fun and no one caught my cold.

When we got home I took Benadryl. It helped but the next day my arthritis was awful. I had forgotten how much Benadryl dries you out. In spite of that we did grocery shopping, washed the car, and bought an electric mixer for the kitchen. All we had was a hand mixer and that was too hard on my arthritis and took forever when you wanted to whip cream.

"I want seconds on your chicken and dumplings. I really like them." Reiny said as he got up and went to the stove to help himself to some more. He kissed my cheek as he went by.

"I won't have to take all your lady friends, (our table mates at the home) to that chicken and dumpling place off I-80 now, as yours are better than what that restaurant makes."

He informed me with a wink. His winks were so cute. He didn't learn to wink as a lad, so when he winked, he screwed his whole face up. It always made me laugh.

"Let's take some dumplings to our neighbors down the street as Donna isn't feeling well."

"Sure I'll take some down just as soon as I finish eating the rest of this bowl. Do save some for us for leftovers," he pleaded.

The next day we did eat the left overs and Reiny was happy. I was too, as the temperature was 102*. That's too hot to cook.

"Oh no, my back is starting to hurt again. Maybe they will give me those shots so I can avoid back surgery. Let's find out?"

We did and they wouldn't do it but scheduled me for back surgery.

Meanwhile Reiny wanted to renew his driver's license. I had heard that Aumsville was easier and less crowded than Salem DMV. We went over there. Unfortunately, they demanded too many papers that we didn't have, so we ended up back in Salem.

We were at the DMV and took a number at 8:30 but didn't get called 'till 12:00. It was too late for Reiny to take his test. I however was able to change my name on my driver's license. Reiny was upset he didn't get to take his test. That evening he got cranky. That was a first. I told him I guessed the honeymoon was over after just one month.

Married Life Comes With Relatives

It was the day of Summer Dawn's shower to be held in Vancouver, Washington. We drove up right after church. Reiny's driving scared me. He saw nothing wrong. That scared me even more, as he had just made a left turn from not the left turn lane, but from two lanes over on the right. We could have had a bad wreck.

"But I wanted to go left" was his only excuse. He had temporarily forgotten where he wanted to go and thus got into the wrong lane.

It was nice meeting more of Reiny's family. The hostess for the shower sat by me and we visited. Then out of the blue she ask me,

"Why did you marry Reiny?"

She must not know him very well, I thought. Maybe she knew the 'old' Reiny and not the one I had now.

"Because I fell in love with him." I replied. "He is a very nice gentleman, and fun to be with."

On the way home I told Reiny what she had said and he ask,

"Why didn't you ask her why she married her husband?"

When we got back home Donna, our neighbor, brought us a coffee cake. The next morning we ate it like a vacuum cleaner. It was very good.

With the nice coffee cake in his tummy, Reiny tried to take his driver's license test again, but failed. After you fail three times you have to wait 6 months before you can take it again. Reiny's license would have expired by then. He was so discouraged.

"Help me understand this driver's manual so I can pass my test. Ask me questions, would you?" Reiny handed me the pamphlet and sat himself in the double recliner.

"Of course, I'll be glad to help. Let's start at the beginning and just go slow."

We spent many a night studying that driver's manual. The next time he took it, however, he failed again. One question he missed was, "What would you do if there was a deer on the side of the road?" The answer was, slow down and watch. He put "stop". She told him if he did that someone might run into him. I was so glad she said that as Reiny did indeed "stop" on the highway or road if he didn't know if he should turn or not. He didn't pull over to the side of the road to do his thinking. I just knew we would be rear ended but luckily we never were.

He never was able to get his license and when his expired I had to do all the driving. I think he missed driving, as it made him feel "macho." We would just have to find other ways to make him feel "macho." He really didn't complain a whole lot. However, he did love telling me how to drive until I threatened to put a sack over his head. Then he found other things to talk about.

Beach Time

It was time for Reiny's family reunion at Beverly Beach. After a nice breakfast at I-Hop we headed for the coast. We checked into our hotel. (We weren't going to 'tent' it) Then we headed to the beach to find the kids campsite. As we were early we could visit with each family as they arrived. They filtered in all day. Many of them I had not met yet. It turned out to be quite a challenge to remember everyone's name as about 26 came. They ranged in ages from 2 yrs. old to 88 yrs. old. It was so fun!

Vicki, (the organizer of the reunion) brought chicken soup for all, and we ate at 7:30 p.m. The rest of the evening was spent visiting. As Reiny was used to going to bed early, we left by nine, and went back to the motel.

"The mirror in our bathroom is off the wall." A gruff voice that I perceived was my husband, announced. I could tell he was unhappy.

"This motel is cheap, clean, and quiet." I reminded him. "Just come to bed," and he did. We slept well.

The next morning we went back to the beach for a nice breakfast of biscuits on a stick, scrambled eggs, juice and coffee.

Lunch was catch as catch can then at 4:30 Reiny started to fry chicken wings and salmon that we brought. It was sooooo good. Everyone liked it. His two granddaughters helped him. He enjoyed that.

He didn't finish cooking until 7:30 and had stood the whole time. His back hurt for two days afterward.

"That's the last time I am going to do that. They will have to change their menu." How prophetic he was.

The grandkids and great grandkids took good care of us and helped us to the beach. They carried chairs so we didn't have to try and get up and down off a blanket. That was really nice. It was a nice day. All the great grandkids were so cute and nice to us.

We slept good at the motel and watched a preacher on T V before going to the beach for breakfast. I ate cold left over chicken wings but Reiny got biscuits and gravy. We visited until noon and headed home. Ate left over chicken wings for supper and were in bed and sleeping by 8:00. We slept the clock around. Reiny brought coffee to bed at 8:30 the next morning. We were to go up and see my Tim's new house but my pain was too severe, I took a strong pain pill and rested.

Operation

"**R**einy, please come kill this monster spider for me. It's in the shower"

"I'll be right there; just let me get my shot gun"

He made me laugh just visualizing that. He did kill the thing without the use of his shot gun. If he had used the shot gun we might not have been able to hear the phone.

The call we had been waiting for finally came.

"Your back surgery date will be October 13th. You must be there at eleven and surgery at one." I hoped it wasn't Friday the 13th. (It wasn't)

I called and talked to the hospital nurse about my surgery. We went in and had all the preliminary things done, like the E K G, blood work, and x rays. I had to be fitted for a corset like thing that was tightened with Velcro. I would wear that for three months. When we got everything done I wondered if time would crawl by now. I am so anxious for the operation.

I spent days making Reiny's favorite cookies and special dishes and freezing them for when I would be recovering. It helped the time fly by. Reiny and I played Wii bowling to pass the time and it was fun. We both enjoyed it a lot.

My special friend, Erlaine, from out of town, made a special trip down to see me and we went out to lunch. We had a great time. It's so nice to have super girl pals. I love marriage but female friends just understand one's feelings better.

Reiny got his hair cut back over where we used to live; so we stayed there for lunch. We had lots of laughter, as usual. Ginny, my dear friend, and Reiny were playing around and teasing. She ended up sitting on his lap. He was afraid I would be mad, but I just laughed and told her to

"Get off, I saw him first."

After lunch he dropped me off at my Beauty Parlor. He went shopping for groceries. Nice distribution of work, don't you think? He will do a good job of taking care of me after the hospital, I'm sure.

As we pulled up our driveway in Turner, we both exclaimed at the same time,

"Look, someone has mowed our lawn for us while we were gone."

"We live in such a caring neighborhood," Reiny said.

After I was home from the hospital he would find this to be so true, as the neighbors all took turns bringing us a meal a day.

It was Saturday and I started having only liquids to prepare for Monday's surgery. Reiny took me to a movie to make the time fly by faster and take my mind off things.

Sunday's sermon was so perfect. It was about 'God Has A Plan." After church my longtime friends Pat and Betty from Corvallis, came up and brought marmalade, jelly beans, apple pie, and cookies. Reiny fixed fried chicken wings, mashed potatoes and gravy, plus tomato slices. He did dishes too. My lady friends thought he was a keeper for sure. I did too.

This is the day! Reiny got me to the hospital early. No surprise there. The surprise came when the surgery was to be at one and it actually got started before that.

I came out of the anesthetic about seven but remember very little. I did remember the pretty bouquet of flowers Vicki brought me and a cuddly pink pig Reiny brought me, plus an 'I Love You' balloon too. My cousin, Ila, checked in with me too. She lives in the next town over so that was very nice of her to come.

Two men came in and turned me over every two hours throughout the night in order to prevent blood clots.

"Ouch that hurts!"

The men informed me it was very necessary, so just put up with it. (That's my translation. They said it nicely, of course.)

The surgeon said she had to do more than she thought she was going to have to do. My incision is 8 inches by 3 inches. The doctor said I would hate her for six months then love her in a year. That was about it, all right.

The next day after surgery was pretty much lost from my memory, due to pain pills, no doubt. I do remember Betty and Delores, and Jerry from the church came to see me. Reiny and Vicki came too.

I slept so much Reiny finally just left in the early afternoon. I certainly didn't blame him for leaving.

There are so many muscles in your back that have to be pulled and stretched to put the rods in. No wonder they scream at you. Mine certainly had good lungs, I heard them screaming loud and clear.

The day dawned bright and clear but I wasn't. This is the day you begin to wonder if it is really worth it. Pain was setting in as if it was a permanent boarder. I had a fever and my blood pressure was so low it caused me to be dizzy. I wasn't eating but finally decided to try a few bites of an egg sandwich. Nope, it didn't want to stay down, and didn't.

"I feel lousy" I lamented to my poor patient husband.

Reiny had come at 10:30 in the morning and hadn't left. It was now 4:30 and he was going home. He was so sweet. What would I do without him?

The next day he brought me yellow roses and lots of cards from our friends. I was still running a fever so all his attention really helped take my mind off of the pain and fever. He was so happy each time a nurse hugged or made over the cute cuddly little pig he had given me. He had gone against his daughters wishes when he bought it for me but he thought it was so cute. I still keep it on my bed to this day. It makes me smile just to look at it.

Operation Recovery

"You may go home by 9:30 this morning." The nurse said as she removed everything that was attached to my body.

I immediately called Reiny and told him, but at 10:15, he was not there. I was surprised. So I called him again.

"I'm sorry, time got away from me. I'm over at Tami's house, (his youngest daughter). He was playing with his great granddaughter. What a cutie she is. I could see how time could fly by.

He came right over and we started home. He was very considerate and drove smoothly, so as not to hurt my back. This was not his usual way of driving, and I had dreaded the trip home.

I hurt all day but was so grateful not to be in rehab but at home with Reiny. I hoped he would not be sorry that he had asked me to wait until we were married to have the operation.

The next day, Saturday, I had nausea, pain, fatigue and fever. Our neighbor brought over bean soup, barbeque spare ribs, and a roast for Sunday.

That helped not only Reiny but me as well, because I didn't need to worry about feeding Reiny.

"I'll stay home too and we'll worship together with a T V preacher today."

We did and he fixed communion, we read the Bible and he prayed. I was so proud of him.

We were both so thankful, Tim, my eldest son, came down from Portland and changed my old bandage for a new fresh one. He also brought a shower stool and put it together. That will help a lot. Tim's wife, Tami, daughter, Taylor, and son, Dan, and Dan's finance, Megan, also came. We had a great visit. They made the time go by nicely in spite of my persistent fever.

Reiny wanted to visit his dog and take his daughter, Tami, out to lunch, plus do some errands. I was feeling dizzy, due to meds, so I called my cousin, Ila. She drove over and spent the time with me, plus changed our sheets and cleaned them. That was so helpful. After she left our neighbor, Elsie, brought us a meatloaf supper. This is the same neighbor that makes the Coca Cola cake that melts in your mouth.

Reiny came home with a "Mr. Coffee" machine. He usually makes the coffee but we will both enjoy it.

Reiny brought me my "Percocet". He had a hard time getting it as our usual drug store was out of it and he had to go hunt elsewhere. I took it and in two hours my pain was gone and the dizziness too. Wow, that was wonderful and worth the trouble he had to go through to get it.

That night I slept like a log but Reiny threshed and kicked his legs, all night. When I mentioned it in the morning, he said,

"I was just doing my exercises."

We were being so blessed by our generous neighbors. Mary Lou, who lived just down the street, brought us steamed spinach, squash, cord' n blue, and tomatoes. Reiny was so nice and let me eat all the spinach myself. I enjoyed it so much.

(Remember, he doesn't like vegetables, so the sacrifice wasn't too great.)

I needed help in getting dressed and Reiny gladly helped. He made me laugh so much. I'm glad it didn't hurt to laugh. One day as we were trying to pull on my panties he said,

"I've helped many a lady take off her panties, but never helped anyone put them on, till now."

That made me laugh. His daughter said when I shared that with her,

"He's just bragging."

"Here comes Orris from down the street with our supper. I'll get the door." Reiny beamed.

He had brought us a wonderful chicken casserole, salad and apple crisp. I wondered if Reiny would be happy with my cooking when I had to cook again. He was certainly enjoying the neighbor's food. He cleaned their dishes and returned them the next day.

"Oh honey, I'm so sorry but I must have twisted wrong."

It was only 3:00 a.m. I was crying and sobbing and Reiny was holding me and trying to calm me down. In the morning I thanked him and he said he didn't even remember doing it.

All that neighbor food was keeping his strength up. The next day our neighbors, George and Mabel

Rice, brought Chicken Tetrazzini and Reiny ate three helpings. The brownies were appreciated by his tummy also. The Lydas brought us our last wonderful meal. Now we would have to go it on our own. Reiny and I had so appreciated the help while I was getting better.

Winter Coming On

A Fireplace, Mocha, and Reiny in the morning; who could ask for anything more. When we woke up this morning, I felt frisky. I held on to Reiny's arm as he started to get up so he couldn't get up. We had a tug a war until I started laughing so hard I grew weak and he won. He had grown weak too, probably because I was so strong, or perhaps because he was laughing so hard too. He plopped back in bed to rest. I took my feet and started to push him out of bed. He managed to get up just before he would have fallen on the floor.

As we were drinking coffee by the fire he said,

"I'm so glad I married you. I had no idea marriage could be so much fun!"

I felt the same way.

When he went to get groceries later on in the day he might have felt differently. He forgot the checkbook, he didn't remember the code to his debit card, and didn't have enough cash. They kept the groceries while he went to his bank and got cash, came back and collected the groceries. They had put the two boxes of ice cream in a freezer and forgot to get them out for him. He never made it home with his ice cream.

Watching the World Series helped him forget his troubles.

"You really smell good. You look mighty handsome today too. Mother will appreciate you sitting by her at church today."

I prayed the Lord would bless him today. It shouldn't be too much longer before I can go with him to church. We put chicken in the oven before he left and I slept the whole time he was gone.

My cousin Ila bought us a mattress cover and then changed the sheets. Was that ever helpful!

We had a nice visit too. We will eat Thanksgiving dinner with she and her husband, at a German restaurant in Woodburn.

"The doctor told me not to feel badly about still having pain as she cut a lot of muscles, bone, tissue and nerves. She has increased my pain meds. I am anemic also."

"It will all go away soon." Reiny tried to encourage me.

Just then the doorbell rang and our neighbor, Donna, handed us another casserole. That was timely as I was having a bad day and that was so appreciated.

When it was my mother's 99th birthday all the relatives in the area met at Red Lobster. My son, Tim, picked Mother up and brought her over to the restaurant to celebrate. I was hurting too badly to go back to her place for the cake, but the rest of them did.

I was in bed by seven. Reiny's sympathy helps a lot. The next day Reiny again had to go to church alone. I was so proud of him. When he got home my friends, Pat and Marge had come up from Corvallis and brought soups and breads. Oh so good. Then they surprised us with apple crisp too. What would we do without such good friends?

Today my sweetie tried to pouch eggs. It was a disaster.

"We better wait until you are up and about before we try that again." He snickered.

Today Mr. Obama became our president. We'll see how time plays that out.

"Honey, I think our marriage is wonderful," Reiny said as he sat down next to me on our double recliner.

"This romance of ours, in the old folk's home, turned out pretty good." I answered him sweetly. We had both learned that to love and be loved is the greatest joy in the world!

"Honey, I'm sorry but I feel cranky today. This is my day to show my flip side. I hope you can live with it." I warned Reiny.

Reiny knew that my friends, Ginny, Lenore and Vesta, were coming over so he put on some good smelling after shave.

"I shaved twice today" he announced. *He is so funny*, I thought. I knew he was looking forward to hugging the women. He enjoyed that a lot. Today was a good day for it beings as how I was cranky.

The ladies came and we visited for 2 hours. We gave Lenore the pickled onions that we had bought for her while we were on our honeymoon. I gave

Ginny a "Princess" book like what I have and enjoy so much, and we gave a gold ringed mug to Vesta.

They invited us to the Thanksgiving dinner at the retirement home the next Saturday. Reiny quickly accepted.

Their visit had helped me get over being cranky. Reiny was glad for that.

Here Comes the Holidays and Relatives

"I know it's early but please open the package on the table." I could tell Reiny was so excited. He just couldn't wait for me to open his package.

"Oh, it's just beautiful. I have never had anything so beautiful before." A diamond bracelet was shining up at me.

"I'll help you put it on and you can wear it to church today."

I did that and he kept taking my arm and showing everyone my 'early' Christmas present. He was so proud of himself. I felt very loved. Reiny wanted the world to know that he loved me.

Sometimes when you marry in your old age you have to remember that not only do our bodies get old but the mind does too. No one likes to believe this. One night I woke at 3:30 a.m. and heard water running. I made my way to the sound and found a faucet on full blast; the hand bowl was running over onto the floor. If you're sleepy and deaf you wouldn't notice. I cleaned up the mess and Reiny never knew it. That was a small price to pay for all the love he gave to me.

Christmas was coming and so many things were going on. We had a lot of happenings to choose from.

"Let's go to that other retirement home where our manager friends have moved to. They are having a Christmas extravaganza. When they invited us we told them we would try and come." Reiny suggested one Sunday afternoon.

"Sounds like fun to me."

It was indeed an extravaganza. We were welcomed by our friends and taken to the 4th floor where they were putting Rum on ice-cream. The

3rd floor had chocolate cake and pastries. The 2nd floor had a chocolate fountain where you could dip strawberries, marshmallows and cookie dough. Such choices one had to make. It was fun. It was so nice to see "old" friends and visit. We found that getting home felt mighty good to us too. Neither one of us was a party animal anymore.

I had stopped taking my pain pills. I found I had a window of 15 minutes before my pain started. I wanted to get my hair done so I hurriedly put a rib roast with onions, carrots and potatoes in the oven. Then Reiny drove me to my hair appointment. When he picked me up he informed me that his grandkids, Mark and Sherry were passing through and would be having supper with us. They brought an almond cake. That was nice as I had all the rest of the dinner ready. We enjoyed them very much in spite of my pain. I liked all his family.

"When we combined our families we sure got a lot of birthdays, didn't we?" I said as I finished wrapping great grandson 'Oliver's" present. I had just written a check and put it in a birthday card for my grandson, Ivan.

"Do we have even one month free of birthdays now?" Reiny wanted to know.

"I'm afraid not, sweetie." I answered as we headed for the car to go celebrate Oliver's party at the pizza place.

My pain prevented us from staying too long at the party. Reiny grabbed some cake to take home in one hand, and held my hand with his other. He certainly was taking good care of me. He is so considerate. *He is a nice man,* I thought. In spite of my pain, we laugh a lot.

I enjoy rehab as I love to swim. I don't mind exercising in the pool. Reiny takes me, then goes visits his dog for a short time, and comes gets me. We then eat out. Reiny and I seem to really enjoy each other's company and talk and visit as long-time friends. It is wonderful to be loved so much.

No Electricity

The temperature dipped into the teens. When I opened the drapes one morning the world was all white and snow was falling like a white out. It didn't matter. Reiny and I sat by our fire, drinking our coffee and chatting away. Later on in the morning I said,

"It seems extra cold this morning. Is our furnace running?"

I wrapped a blanket around me and cuddled in the big recliner.

"The TV isn't working either" Reiny complained.

"I think our electricity has gone out. Good thing we got our coffee and took our showers before it went out. They will probably have it on in an hour or so. Would you like some cold cereal for breakfast?"

"I can get that for us. You just stay under the blanket" Reiny said as he headed for the kitchen.

During the morning we talked on our phones to our kids and grandkids. For lunch grandsons, Josh, and Jordy, brought chicken sandwiches and orange juice from Mc Donalds . There was still no electricity by night, so we had a spoonful of left over unhardened fudge for supper.

Not bad. I realize we were missing vegetables, but chocolate does come from beans, remember.

We visited all evening. I found out all about Reiny's relatives, and his early childhood. Before the electricity came on I heard all about his life from the cradle to when I met him. His kids seem to have a different version, so they will need to write that book. It certainly was interesting to me. He had had a hard life but it seemed to me he had made the best of what he had been dealt.

We went to bed early to get warm, and did.

There was still no electricity in the morning when we woke up.

"So much for my Mocha this morning." I lamented while I washed my face and body with ice cold water. Believe me that will wake you up.

"I'll walk down the hill and get you a Mocha from that little drive thru coffee shack on the corner."

"Oh no, please don't! I don't want to have a husband with a broken leg or arm. With my back I couldn't take care of you. Besides, by the time you would bring it back up the hill, it would be cold. Thanks for offering, though."

The snow had stopped by noon but we still had no electricity. Gary, one of our neighbors, braved the roads and picked us up. He took us down the hill to the dining area of the Turner retirement home, where mother lived. We had a nice lunch and got warm. We were able to plug in our telephones too.

In the afternoon grandson Josh brought us over a two burner propane camping stove. We were all set now. In order to use it safely we had to set it up in the garage, bundle up, and open the garage door, to let out the fumes.

It snowed off and on all day. Reiny fried things from the freezer that were defrosting. I was always told that if you didn't open your freezer, things would stay frozen for several days. That is simply NOT TRUE!

"I see lights on down the street. Our end of the street seems to be the only place without electricity." I said as I called the electrical company again. Cell phones were a blessing.

"They said there might not be power until next week. Oh dear! This is our third day now without electricity. Several people have invited us to go to their house, or we can go down to the main building. Our neighbors are moving in with their friend down the hill. We will be alone up here. What do you think, sweetie?"

"Let's just tough it out. I like it here with just you and me. But I will take you to a motel or we can see if the guest room at the retirement center where we used to live is available; if you don't want to stay up here and tough it out." *He is so considerate*, I thought.

The doorbell rang so our conversation ended for now.

"Hi, I brought you a battery camping lamp."

Our neighbor, Beverly, was so considerate. We visited for a while, and then noticed our kitchen floor was flooding. Our freezers were defrosting. Beverly left as Reiny and I started mopping up the water. The freezer in the garage had defrosted too.

Good thing Reiny had put the ice-cream in a casserole with a tight fitting lid, and stuck it out in the snow. The temperature was still in the teens so the ice cream didn't melt. The bread did not fare as well, as the animals were able to get to it. We unwillingly shared our freezer contents with the raccoons and birds and whatever other animals heard about the feast the Zoller's were serving in their back yard.

"It's only one day more until Christmas eve. Let's open our presents now."

Reiny was worse than I was about waiting.

"O k, I'll go first." I said as I watched him quickly bring me a box. It was a jewelry size box. I opened it carefully and there was a beautiful topaz necklace.

"Thank you, darling, but you already gave me a diamond bracelet a few days ago. You truly spoil me. I'm glad I married you."

He had several packages to open. He got the slippers that he wanted, a shirt, and some other items he had asked for.

"You only got to open one present and I had several. That's not fair."

"Oh, honey, my one present was far more costly than all of yours combined."

"After Christmas I want to take you to Macy's so you can get a new purse. The one you have now has been repaired several times. You need a new one. Don't argue."

"I wouldn't dream of it" I smiled. *There would be after Christmas sales going on then too,* I thought.

Christmas and No Electricity?

It was December 24th and still no electricity. We had to throw out everything we had in the freezers and fridge. It was the fourth day now of freezing temperatures and we were still without a furnace.

"The lights are back on!" we both shouted at once. It was 4:00 pm. Christmas eve.

We had been invited for Christmas dinner by neighbors, Keith and Helena, whose electricity came on before ours did. We were going to go. Several of us 'Hill Toppers' enjoyed Christmas dinner together. We each had stories to tell about our time without electricity. The time flew by. Reiny drove through the left over snow, down the hill, and picked up mother. She would spend Christmas with us.

"This was a different Christmas but very pleasant." I told Reiny as we prepared for bed that night.

The next day we took all the Christmas decorations down. We watched T V and both were very glad to have the electricity back on once again.

While visiting on the phone with a friend from where we used to live, we found out that one of our friends, Ruth, had fallen and broke her hip. That happens so often. Ruth was a really nice lady but not strong enough to survive a broken hip and she died. This really shocked us. We were both so sorry. She had helped Reiny with his dog as she had a dog also. Having so many "old" friends has a down side to it. We found out another of our table mates had died while we were gone.

We were feeling badly when Reiny's daughter, Vicki, and her husband rang the doorbell. They brought us a Christmas present. It was a thoughtful one as Reiny and I often sit in the recliner and watch out the patio door at the birds. They gave us a round bird feeder, bird seeds, and a book of Oregon birds. We used that bird book at least once a day until the day we moved. Reiny made sure the bird feeder was always full of seeds.

"It's so fun watching the squirrels trying to get the bird seed and stay away from the cats at the same time." I told Reiny.

A big cat was walking past our sliding door, stopped and peeked in at us. It made me laugh. Reiny slowly walked over to the cat, so as not to scare it, squatted down and talked with him. He didn't let him in, because I have allergies. The cat turned its head from side to side as if talking with Reiny too,

New Year's Eve came and went. We didn't wait to watch the ball drop in New York. Little did I know I had just spent my first and last Christmas and New Years with Reiny! I don't think we would have done anything any differently if we had known it was our last together.

The snow is continuing now in 2009, in spite of that my sister and her husband came down and we all ate at the Red Lobster restaurant.

"I like your sister's real black hair." Reiny told me later on in the day after they had gone back home.

Do you want me to dye mine?" I ask him.

"Oh No! I wouldn't know you. I like you just the way you are, white hair and all."

"Good thing." I wasn't about to fool with coloring my hair and trying to keep the white roots from showing. *Just because his hair still has a lot of color in it still,* I thought.

A Short Time Of Good health

Three days into the New Year my son, Tim, and his family, came from Portland with all the equipment to deep fry a Turkey. WOW! Was it good! I had made cowboy beans, fruit salad, and pies. One of Tim's sons, Dan and his finance, Megan came too. We had a wonderful belated Christmas.

The next day I went to get a turkey leg I had saved just for me and found that Reiny had eaten it all. I was disappointed and made a big fuss. When we went to bed I sat up and watched T V. A little childish, you're thinking? Well, old age comes with a second childhood too.

I am getting worried. Reiny seemed unable to hear or pay attention today. When we came out of a store, he couldn't find the car. I realize that happens to all of us at one time or another but even when I told him what row it was in, and how many spaces down it was, he still couldn't find it. Something was not right with him.

Reiny had an appointment at the V A hospital. It would be the first of many, many we would have this year. I don't like the V A hospital because you get a different doctor every time. They seem to have a hard time figuring out what's going on.

We drove over to the coast to relax and enjoy some time on the beach with Vicki and Maur at their Condo. We had to fill out a lot of V A papers and Annuity papers. I did it on the beach. Vicki fixed a delicious dinner for us, in spite of a bad tooth ache and taking pain pills. What a gal!

I drove home but we didn't make it by dark. I don't like to drive in the dark anymore. Bed felt good. We both are too old and our health isn't as good as we'd like, so these one day trips just are too hard on us anymore.

Our dish washer spewed out water all over the kitchen floor.

"Help" I yelled to Reiny. "I need help"

"Call 911" was his reply.

He thinks he is so funny. (And he is)

I cleaned up the counters all spiffy after his daughter Tami and her son, Josh and family ate lunch with us. After they had left I walked into the kitchen and noticed a cup turned over on my clean counter. I wondered who put it there?

"Eeeeek" A cute little tree frog jumped out at me when I lifted the cup. He startled me. I grabbed for him but he was too fast. I noticed Reiny watching with a big grin on his face.

"Please come help me catch this little fellow. He is fast."

Reiny walked over and reached his hand down to pick him up, as if there was nothing to it. I began to laugh as the frog played 'leap frog' with him too and the frog was definitely winning. I joined back in the game until Reiny finally caught him. He walked outside and placed the frog back on the tree where he had gotten the little fellow.

It was February and we both were feeling healthy. This would be a rare happening at our house. You don't take anything for granted when you get old. We appreciated our good health.

Reiny's daughter, Vicki, was going to be baptized at her church in Portland. We were invited and certainly wanted to go.

Reiny was up by 5:15 a m, shaved, showered and ready to go by 6:00. He fixed coffee to hurry me up. We did leave at 7:15. In spite of eating breakfast in Woodburn, we still got there 2 ½ hours early. I wasn't going to sit out in the church parking lot that long, so we drove to a mall and went shopping. Reiny got a velour sport jacket, two shirts, and a sweater. I didn't find anything. It didn't matter as I had plenty of 'things'.

The baptism was lovely. They chanted and sang the scriptures. Vicki was so pretty and all smiles. To celebrate she had invited friends to meet her afterwards at a nice Mexican restaurant. The food was so good, but Reiny hardly ate anything. This was the first sign of his deadly illness, but we didn't know it yet.

Reiny wanted to go to the Dakota's to celebrate our first anniversary. It was still four months away but he wanted to get tickets to the outdoor amphitheater. They put on a play once a year.

"They come from all over the world to see this. The tickets might sell out." He worriedly told me.

So I went to the computer to see what he was talking about. I could tell we needed to get our tickets soon. I called my ticket person, Tim's wife, Tami. I gave her all the information and she took care of it all for us. She even got the tickets for the famous 'STEAK ON A STICK' dinner. Reiny wanted to be sure we got to that.

He was so excited he called his sister to see if she couldn't join us. She lived just a few hundred miles away from where the outdoor show took place. She was able to get a room in the motel we were to be in. Our plans were all working out until we discovered there was no airport close by where we wanted to go, nor did the bus stop close by, or did the train. We had to do some more thinking.

This was a problem. If we were to drive, I had a problem.

"I'm sorry, honey, but with my congestive heart failure problem I can't stay very long in altitudes over three thousand feet. The map shows Montana has very few such places where we could spend the night. I couldn't drive all across Montana at one time. Now what should we do?" We had to do some more thinking.

The V A Hospital (our second home)

Meanwhile we went up to the V A hospital again and again. We finally asked if some of the tests could be done at the satellite V A office here in Salem. It turned out that 'yes,' that was possible .So we did that every time we could.

Reiny was so happy when it was his turn to host his six grown grandkids for a night of poker. They all came over to the house, brought a Pizza, and played poker. Reiny lost, but he didn't care. He had so much fun with them. I watched T V in the bedroom. I was happy for him.

The next day he was very happy also as I made kneple soup, like his mother used to make. I never heard of it so he tried to describe it to me. It turned out O K and he was pleased. The next time I asked his sister for the recipe. That helped a lot. Its chicken broth, (and any vegetables you want to sneak in) plus a type of biscuit dough that you pinch off in tiny marble size pieces. These boil in the broth. As he became more and more ill that soup was a big help. I think it was a comfort food for him.

Reiny was feeling well enough to go with me to the wedding of a couple in their 80's. It was held at our church and was so nice. During the ceremony, Reiny whispered to me,

"She is so wrinkled." Reiny liked perfection in women. How he liked me, I don't know.

One of their kids drove them to the beach for a honeymoon. The man could hardly walk, but they laughed a lot, cooked together and seem to have lots of fun. Maybe romance in the later years is even better than in the younger years. You learn what is really important and what isn't worth getting in a snit over. You learn that laughter is what holds two people together.

On Valentine's Day Reiny did not feel good. He gave me a beautiful gold and silver bracelet. I gave him a lamp that turns off and on when you clap. He likes it and used it a lot in the night.

I was so sorry Reiny wasn't feeling well. We were scheduled to go to the V A hospital in Portland and we went as scheduled. I hoped the V A hospital doctors could help him.

It was too much to hope for. They didn't help him at all. It made me so happy that in spite of his illness, he never lost his sense of humor. The next day I hollered in at him,

"I'm leaving for the ladies church group, sweetie, do you need anything?"

"Yes! Get me a babysitter. I want someone to read me a story."

He's so funny. This morning after he did the dishes he complained

"I don't want to go back and visit our old retirement home because all the men will see my dish pan hands."

Mother was at the ladies meeting and brought some chocolates that she made for Reiny. He liked that. Chocolate is about the only vegetable he will eat. (Remember it comes from a bean)

On one of our trips to the VA hospital we stopped at the bowling alley in Vancouver where he had played on a league team. We ate lunch there and he got to see a lot of his "old" cronies. It made him very happy. He told them all that he was a "born again" Christian now. He seemed so happy about that.

"Sweetheart, I want to trade in our cars and just get one. You are the only driver now and I would like to get a big car that will protect you."

I wondered if he felt because I would be the only one driving, that a big car would protect him too.

We looked at several car lots and then went back to where I had bought my car years ago. The same salesman came to wait on us and recognized me or maybe he recognized my car I had bought from him. Reiny told him what we wanted and what we wanted to pay and how we wanted to trade in the two cars. He seemed to understand.

"Let's drive this one, Joanne and Reiny. You'll like it."

I couldn't believe it. It was a 2006 Chrysler touring 300. The tag said, gold, but it looked light brown to me. I fell in love with it. It rode so smoothly. Reiny seemed pleased too and we drove away with our big boat of a car.

Reiny's doctor called from Portland V A hospital and said Reiny had kidney failure. I will take him up to have a catheter put in. He isn't too happy about that. He also has to have a blood test and an ultra sound of his bladder. One thing after another, but sometimes that is life. Could anything more go wrong? YES!

My broker called and said I had lost 92% of my portfolio. The whole country was having the same problem. This was serious stuff. We went to the senior center to get our taxes done and they said,

"It's too complicated for us. Go to an accountant."

So I bundled everything up and sent it to my usual tax accountant.

Reiny had a catheter put in. They were able to do it here in Salem. The plug came out in the night and the contents went all over the rug and bed.

Reiny was not feeling well and got so sick he wanted to go up to the E R at the V A hospital in Portland. That's a good hour's drive and snow was falling gently but not too bad, yet. I fearfully started off for Portland. I got him checked in and then was able to find where I was supposed to park. We ended up having to stay there for seven hours. They finally gave him antibiotic salve and a deadening gel and sent us home. I had begun to worry about the weather. We just made it home before the snow really started coming down hard. A real storm was brewing.

The next day, Sunday, Reiny still wasn't feeling well so I stayed home with him and we worshiped at home. There would be many a Sunday we had to worship at home before he would get to go to his final home.

Reiny is dizzy today and the cap came off his catheter again. What a mess. I took mother to the cardiologist. He said she had had a slight stoke. Her pacemaker wasn't working right.

About this time I was getting very tired and depressed. I figured I needed more time with God, so I took it. He told me through His word that He was with me, and would give me sufficient strength for whatever He asks me to do. With taking Mother to three doctors in three different towns, and taking Reiny to V A offices and doctors and tests and E R in two towns, some 75 miles apart, I felt the Lord came close to giving me more than I could handle. God provided help through our wonderful friends and relatives.

That old saying, "Pressure can burst a pipe or make a diamond." Well, I think my pipe was bursting, but I wanted to be a diamond and sparkle.

We're back to just rain now. I took Reiny to the V A office here and they gave him a new catheter plus some more caps for it.

Then they sent us back to the V A hospital in Portland. There the doctor told us,

"Reiny is having some bad effects from a former cancer operation. He has had three cancer operations and radiation, according to his records."

"No one is paying any attention to the fact that he is losing weight all the time." I told the doctor.

"Of course he is. He is sick." The doctor replied matter-of-factly. *A lot of help that is*, I thought.

We went to the V A office here in Salem but they just made an appointment with the urologist in Portland for April. The same date as Mother had an appointment with her doctor. I changed mother's appointment.

To top off the day, our taxes came. We had to pay $8.000. Wow. I have never had to pay that much, even when I owned a business.

The next day I was blessed, as my friends from all over the state called and encouraged us. What would we do without them? I was cranky and tired and <u>I</u> didn't even like <u>me</u>. Reiny assured me that he still liked me.

What to do? What to do?

Warm weather has finally arrived and it's only April 20th. It got up to 80 degrees today. We enjoyed sitting in our lawn swing and talking to the neighbors as they went by. After watching 'Miss U S A," Reiny now calls me "Miss Turner U S A."

Reiny's 89th birthday was coming up so we headed for the coast to celebrate. Sometimes his brain doesn't seem to be working like it should. He huffs and puffs a lot too. I wonder if he is beginning to show his age.

Reiny was pleased with the great dinner his daughter fixed for him. I gave him his birthday present the evening before his birthday. (Remember, he can never wait.) It was a pair of binoculars. He could find the ships at sea and the birds flying. He seemed quite pleased.

This birthday would be his last here on earth but had we known that, we wouldn't have done anything differently.

By the time we got back home we were both tired and our own bed felt so good.

For the next week we were still tired. We discussed the trip to North Dakota again. He wants me to drive the Motor Home. That didn't seem like a real good idea to me. We need to think some more. Reiny seems to be getting sicker.

Doctors and More Doctors

We took a urine sample to the V A office here in Salem, as they had instructed us. We then headed to the V A hospital in Portland. (Why didn't we just take the urine sample with us to Portland? I wondered that too.)

We got there early and thus were able to get a parking place close to the elevator. We drank coffee in the lobby and recognized some people from our other times there.

They called Reiny almost on time. I kissed him as they rolled him away on the gurney. The operation took over two hours.

The doctor told me,

"We took a mass off his outside artery in his neck. We sent it in for testing."

I was able to take him home that same day. On the way home Reiny said,

"The operation was awful! I'm so glad it is over."

It must have been, as he has never complained before, and he is able to handle a lot of pain. I felt so sorry for him.

The next day Reiny was still not feeling well so I stayed home with him. In Albany, a town close by,

I was supposed to be honored by a church group called "Global Ministries." My sister went to the gathering and said that I was honored in spite of not being there. That was nice.

Reiny complained that he had lost so much weight that he couldn't get his belt tight enough. Something had to be done. I called his Secure Horizon insurance and I will call his Primary Care doctor for an appointment.

We arrived at the V A hospital at 10:30 and drove around and around but couldn't find a parking place. Finely we had to park outside and down the hill.

While they were dripping iron into his arm, I went to check with the finance office. Something didn't seem right to me. We were being billed $1,024 for his operation and $50 each visit. We were scheduled for eight visits this month alone.

They gave me papers to fill out to update their records.

"Well, I see what's wrong. We are using Reiny's former wife's income not yours. We will update our records and bring in your receipts and you will get a refund. " The lady at the desk informed me.

I did bring the receipts to them and they wrote me a check while I stood there. We were never billed again except for small co-pay on his prescriptions.

May arrived and Mother's Day, but Reiny was not feeling well. He is taking lots of pain pills. I bet it is those iron infusions that are affecting him.

Here we go again, back up to the V A hospital to a oncology doctor. The doctor said Reiny's anemia was worse but he stopped the iron infusions and took him off all his pills anyway. They did give him more blood. They noted his weight was way down.

Reiny was weak, dizzy and nauseas today. Poor fellow. I went to a teachers meeting at church as they have ask me to teach a class. Before I left Reiny told me he was going to put the garbage out to the curb.

No honey, this is just Sunday and they don't pick it up until Tuesday."

When I got home he had put the garbage out to the curb anyway.

The doctor in Vancouver V A called and wants me to bring Reiny up there for a chest X ray and more blood tests.

"They take so much of my blood, no wonder I'm anemic." He laughed.

I found out Reiny's mother, two brothers, a sister, and a nephew, all died of cancer. I am very worried. I want to take him to a regular doctor, not those at the V A that keep moving somewhere else. You never get the same doctor twice there. Reiny won't even consider my suggestion. The V A is the only place for him, he told me.

After being sick to his stomach and aching clear thru to his back all the month of June, Reiny allowed me to check on some local doctors. Vicki recommended her doctor and got him an appointment. Reiny was down to 162 lbs. He couldn't believe it.

"Your kidneys are not telling your bones to make red corpuscles. We can do it in the lab now but it is very expensive so you better stay with the V A. I'll give you stronger medication for your stomach." The new doctor said to us.

That is not what we wanted to hear at all. Now what to do?

Reiny took the stronger stomach medicine but it didn't help him. He was still having lots of pain and nausea. I called our new doctor and told him about Reiny still hurting so he set up a time to give him a stomach test. I feel that should have been done in the end of February when he first started throwing up. Now we were well into June.

Decisions Must Be Made

Reiny's son, Phil, and his wife, Sherry, came to visit from Washington. What a great opportunity to get to know them. They stayed two days. We all had the best visit ever.

After a bad night of pain, kicking and jerking and a bad day, Reiny said,

"I don't want to do it, but I think we better cancel our trip to the Dakota's. I am just not well enough to help you."

I knew that was a hard decision for him. He wanted to show me his 'growing up' place.

"Perhaps next year, sweetheart." I answered him. We both knew that was not to be, but we had to hold on to hope. I called and cancelled the reservations and we sadly called his sister and told her.

As we had not heard from the V A hospital about his last blood tests, I called the nurse.

"Reiny's blood count was just 28 and it should be at least 40." She informed me, but she didn't know what they were going to do about it. They would call us.

It was the first night of our churches' State convention. It was being held at the tabernacle in Turner. We picked up Mom and all attended. Reiny and Mom could not hear and it was very hot in there. Reiny said he was not going back. I don't blame him. I was asked to give a presentation and I did, but Reiny did not go. I missed him.

My son, Mike, showed up by 9:00 a m, ate one of my cinnamon rolls then took me to town and bought a gadget that allowed me to talk on my cell phone in the car without using my hands. He set it up for me and taught me how to use it.

After we got home Mike mowed the lawn, trimmed and blew off the patio. The yard looked good. Reiny was very pleased as he could no longer keep it up. We were all pleased when Tim's boy, Dan, and his girl, Megan, came over to visit and eat watermelon with us. I am so blessed that Reiny enjoys my side of the family as much as I enjoy his. Reiny said,

"In spite of me feeling bad. This was a good day."

Reiny was ill all night. I got up by six and went outside and sat on the lawn swing. Mike started to leave at seven but saw me, came over to the swing, and visited with me. He told me he had just had the best year of his life with his girlfriend, Carol. He plans to ask her to marry him. I wish them both happiness for life.

When Reiny and I married we both were aware that, at our age, marriage could come with health issues. No one is ever prepared but we were not surprised either. Reiny and I figured we should be able to have ten years, and that would be alright. Now that possibility didn't seem very realistic anymore.

Reiny's grandson, Josh, set us up with Wii bowling. That proved to be a fun game and Reiny and I enjoyed passing the time playing it. It didn't matter who won. He could play it even as he got weaker and weaker. He didn't stand but just threw from his chair.

Reiny enjoyed playing Wii bowling with my granddaughter, Taylor when she came with her family. It quickly became his game of choice to play with anyone who would play with him.

Mother fell so I took her to the doctor and for an x ray. She had broken a bone but it was in her toe. She hit her head but that seemed to be o k. When I got home Reiny wanted to talk.

A Last Move?

"I think we ought to move back to our former retirement home, where we met. I am getting worse and you will need help caring for me. We have a lot of friends there to support us too. I cannot even go down the driveway to get our mail anymore."

It did seem like a good idea. I would not have to leave him home alone to get groceries. We both would miss our neighbors and our friendly church.

We signed papers and put money down on our new apartment back where we used to live. We would be on the ground floor this time in the main building, instead of in the cottages.

There were some things we just couldn't take with us, so Tim and Tami came from Portland, took pictures of our stuff and sold them on Craig's list on the internet. That was very helpful.

"Here we go a moving again." I sang as I began to pack. We took Reiny's clothes over to the new place, stopped and got some U Haul boxes. Reiny was able to put them together for me. He gets cold and it is 91 degrees outside. I am sweating.

Reiny gets worse every day and feels awful. Today for the first time he got 'sharp'. I think it is because he can't do what he wants to do. Making a move is not easy when you're feeling good, let alone if you are ill.

Over the week-end Tim, Tami, and Taylor came down from Portland and took our bed apart and set it up at the new place. Then they helped us pack. Ila, my cousin, brought cookies to us and stayed to help pack. Tim brought lunch for all of us. Reiny seemed happy to play bowling with Taylor. He does get tired very fast but that is to be expected.

After the Senior Center came and hauled a lot of things away, the old house looked very bare. Reiny was sick, but watched the ball game. By midnight his pain was more than he could bear, so I called 911 and we were off to the E R. They decided he had pancreatitis. That's where the enzymes start eating the pancreas.

He was dehydrated also. We got home by 7 a m. He was scheduled for a CAT scan the next day. Yeah!

We went for the CAT scan and they refused us. They said they hadn't received the authorization from the insurance yet. I sadly took him back home.

Reiny is sick, cranky, and impatient. I try to tread gently. He wants to go stay at the V A hospital. He feels he is dying. He thinks that's where he would be taken care of till he dies, as his twin brother.

The doctor ordered Vitacon for Reiny. I got it, gave it to him, and he began to feel better.

Now to me it is beginning to feel like "same song, second verse." Dale, my second husband, took Vitacon toward the end. It does have goofy type side effects.

Reiny fell, due to the dizziness caused by the pills. I couldn't get him up. I had to call 911. Again we were in the E R until after midnight. He was dehydrated and anemic again.

Reiny had food brought down to our room but ate very little, if anything. When he has company

I run upstairs and eat with my friends. This helps me. I went to church with Ginny. That was helpful too.

Tim, my son, called to check on Reiny and I told him,

"We have boxes everywhere but I'm not going to unload them until after Reiny has his procedure and we talk with the doctor on Wednesday."

"Oh No, Mom. Make a 'home' for Reiny. If he ever needed one, he needs one now." Tim, advised me, when I told him my plans.

I did do that and it made us all feel better. That was good advice.

My grandson, Dan, came over and put up our pictures, one more time. Reiny was fascinated at how carefully he measured and got them up perfectly straight, each time. Reiny was pleased and impressed.

Vicki took out the trash faithfully each time she came, and took home our laundry. What a blessing. She and her husband, Maur, also accompanied me when Reiny had to go to the E R.

The doctor's office called and said,

"Everything was normal on the M R I. We should do it again in four months."

What! I couldn't believe it. What is causing his pain? Doesn't anybody in the medical community care? I was frustrated. I loved this guy and he was suffering. I knew it was hard on his family too.

Reiny's kids, grandkids, and great grandkids were coming to visit. There were as many as 28 in our little room at one time. We had all ages, from 2 to 89 years old. I became worried about my Harp. One of my friends told my concerns to the manager. He came down, picked it up, and took it, via a golf cart, to my friend's house for safe storage. That helped me to relax.

The little ones were playing on the lawn swing and discovered wasps in the side pockets of the swing. Reiny's son, Ray, ran across the street to a hardware store, bought a trap and spray and set it up. It worked. Everyone was relieved.

There just weren't enough days in the week. Mother had cracked her upper plate and needed to go to the dentist to get it fixed. Reiny needed to go to a doctor for two tests. My cousin Ila came through and took my mother to the dentist. Such a blessing.

Our little apartment was beginning to look like a home after I got all the boxes emptied. That made me happy. So many people came to visit. I wouldn't have had it any other way but it was hard to relax.

Reiny Is About Ready to Fly!

Vicki, Ray, and I took Reiny to his procedure. We waited in a little office for the doctor to come in afterwards.

"When is it my turn?" We heard Reiny asking the nurses. He felt he had waited for his tests long enough.

"Mr. Zoller, We have done your tests. You are all through and when the doctor talks to your family, you can go home."

That was so nice that he didn't even know when they did it, as he was so worried.

The doctor came into the little office and sadly told us what the tests showed.

"Reiny won't be with us much longer. His stomach is all cancer. There is nothing we can do."

Two days later a lady from Hospice came to our home to fill out papers. It took four hours and I wasn't sure I was going to make it. Just before she left she ask Reiny,

"Is there anything you want? Do you have a last wish, or want to say anything?"

"Yes" he nodded his head. We were all listening intently.

"I want to be sure Joanne is taken care of after I am gone."

There was silence. What an unselfish man to think of someone else as he was dying.

The hospice lady finally left. As was my custom, I fell apart. Reiny held me and we both cried.

Sharrie, the activity director where we were living, came down with a big platter of cheeses, ham, beef, and pickles plus bread and crackers. That was so considerate. She gave Reiny a big hug and kiss. He liked that. Soon some of his favorite housekeepers, and servers, came down and sat on his bed, visited and gave him hugs. That made him so happy.

Reiny's kids, Phil, Ray, and Vicki, stayed all day. The hospice hygienist gave Reiny a bath, shave, and shampoo. Later on I called grandson, Josh, to help him to the bathroom. Josh was really good with his grandpa.

The hospice nurse came and ordered drugs to be delivered. She wanted to be sure Vicki would be there when they came. The nurse ignored me and kept talking to Vicki. This made me mad. I looked at her and ask,

"Do you <u>not</u> think I am capable of taking care of my husband? I may be old, but my mind is still clear. Please talk to me. I will be giving him the medicine, not his daughter."

Vicki and Maur had a quartet of men come sing around Reiny's bed. What a unique and enjoyable idea that was. Reiny was surprised and pleased.

When kids, grandkids and great grandkids came they played Wii bowling with Reiny. He wasn't really with it, due to his medicine for pain, but he seemed to enjoy playing with them.

The next day Reiny woke up early and wanted his coffee! <u>NOW!</u> Our friend Ginny heard about it and scooted over to Fred Meyers and brought us some instant coffee. That solved the early morning coffee dilemma. What would we do without such good friends?

I heard men's voices talking. Reiny was in the bedroom alone, I thought, and I was reading in the living room. I got up and headed into the bedroom but no one was there but Reiny.

"Who were you talking to, honey?" I was puzzled.

"There were two men standing in the doorway, right about where you're standing. I was talking to them."

Now I knew he was taking strong medicine that might cause hallucinations, but maybe these were his escorts to heaven. I thought. It's possible!

Hospice got a hospital bed for Reiny. He went downhill fast. He went into a kind of coma and soon was gone from us, but still breathing. Vicki was on one side of the bed and I on the other. We held his hands and talked lovingly to him as his breathing became slower and slower and finally just stopped. He had graduated and gone to his final home. I knew he was happier than he had ever been on this earth, but oh I would miss him.

This losing a mate doesn't get any easier at any age. I felt I was loved and had given love.

Yes, in spite of the pain of losing him, Romance in the Old Folks Home was worth it!